Edward Clifford

Father Damien: A Journey From Cashmere To His Home In Hawaii

Edward Clifford

Father Damien: A Journey From Cashmere To His Home In Hawaii

ISBN/EAN: 9783743460836

Manufactured in Europe, USA, Canada, Australia, Japa

Cover: Foto ©Andreas Hilbeck / pixelio.de

Manufactured and distributed by brebook publishing software (www.brebook.com)

Edward Clifford

Father Damien: A Journey From Cashmere To His Home In Hawaii

To the Memory of
LORD MOUNT TEMPLE

I DEDICATE THIS BOOK

WITH him I associate nearly all the best things that have come to me in the last twenty-five years. His intelligent sympathy, his affectionate help, and his faithful prayers have been a stimulus and a reward in all the work that I have tried to do. His influence was so far-reaching that the same testimony might be given by hundreds of persons who, like myself, have learned from him eternal lessons of faith, hope, and love.

E. C.

PREFACE

In giving this short account to the public of FATHER DAMIEN DE VEUSTER and his field of labour, I desire to stir my countrymen in connection with his memory to do their duty in fighting that terrible disease whose victim he was. So practical a man would choose rather than any other reward that through his life and death the evil and misery of the world should be lessened. I tender my hearty thanks to the Editor of the *Nineteenth Century* for allowing me to reproduce three articles of mine which have appeared in that review.

EDWARD CLIFFORD.

CONTENTS

CHAPTER I
INTRODUCTORY 1

CHAPTER II
HAWAIIANS AND HAWAII 30

CHAPTER III
FATHER DAMIEN AND MOLOKAI . . . 45

CHAPTER IV
THE LAKE OF FIRE 133

CHAPTER V
OUR NEXT DUTY 148

I was sick and he visited me

J Bonnier
Venster

Kalavaa Moolotan Dec, 20th 1880

CHAPTER I

INTRODUCTORY

'Thy kingdom come.'

This prayer of Christ's is evidently not yet completely fulfilled, but for all that the kingdom of God is always coming, and even now it is within us and around us.

Wherever faith, purity, and devotion compel the allegiance of men, there is the coming of the kingdom; and wherever love, joy, and peace are reigning, there it has come.

It is no great virtue that we should praise heroes like Father Damien, General Gordon, and Lord Shaftesbury. But it is surely *something*, for in admiring heroes we take the first step towards becoming heroic. Only the first step however, and there are probably many people who never take the second, and who will therefore find themselves very much out in the cold as soon as they die. But we know where it is said, 'Finally, brethren, whatsoever things are true, whatsoever things are honest, whatsoever things are just, whatsoever things are pure, whatsoever things are lovely, whatsoever things are of good report; if there be any virtue, and if there be any praise, think on these things.' Therefore we are not only free to honour such men as Father Damien, but it is even our duty to do so. And it is to be noted that good people have generally a little difficulty at first in quite admiring a hero; for heroes are not made to order, and we cannot get them just on our favourite pattern. None of them are precisely like our grandmothers or our favourite clergymen. Lord Shaftesbury was a party man, General Gordon was unorthodox about everlasting punishment, and Father Damien was a Roman Catholic.

When I was a little boy I thought that all Roman Catholics were wicked, and went steadily to hell. If I saw a nun I thought she wanted to catch me and burn me. The glaring redness of Bloody Mary was unrelieved by any quieter colour.

As I grew older I found I had been mistaken. I read Charles Kingsley's *Hermits*, and the lives of St. Francis and St. Catherine of Sienna. I read *Thomas à Kempis*, and I found that the Church of Rome had undoubtedly produced saints.

A revulsion of feeling often sets in when

young people find that their teachers have not told them the whole truth about religious matters. Unfairness and untruth bring their punishment with the same unerringness as that with which an apple falls to the ground, and often the desire to make amends for past injustice turns the heart towards the Church of Rome, with all its romance and bewitchingness, and against Protestantism, with its gravity and its unbending opposition to certain pleasant errors. Moreover, there are many persons who are more anxious to submit to authority than to question its claims to their obedience. To some it is even a luxury to assent to what they more than half think is untrue. They consider their submission a sacrifice of sense to devotion, forgetting that they are called to worship God with all their mind as well as with all their heart. If their newly chosen guide recommends the delivering up of their Bible, then they willingly let their Bible go. The distress or persecution of friends is but the incentive which finally seals their act and fixes it steadily on the ground of martyrdom. They become earnest disciples, and often they become beautiful souls.

It is not well to dissuade such persons from their secession by any other means than the simple telling of the truth. It is better that they should do what they think is right, even if they find out later that it was wrong, and that they must retrace their steps. The way to truth may be blessedly painful, but it will be trodden sooner or later if the soul loves truth. God teaches slowly.

For myself, I feel that in sending forth this little book I must needs say what the reasons are which prevent my joining the Church of Rome, though my heart is full of love for many of its people, as well as for members of our English Church, and for Wesleyans, Baptists, Congregationalists, Salvation Army people, Plymouth Brethren, Buddhists, heathen, and others too numerous to name. I disagree with many of the doctrines of the Church of Rome, but as I do not suppose that it will turn out that I or any one else in the world is exactly right about every doctrine, I take my stand on principles rather than on even such important questions as prayers for the dead, purgatory, indulgences, schism, everlasting punishment, and modern miracles. Many difficulties as to these matters may be fairly explained, many may be wriggled out of, and many may be maintained if the defender speaks sufficiently loudly and impressively. The following, then, are the principal reasons which prevent my becoming a Romanist, and they may all be read in an ordinary tone of voice. I hope that any Roman Catholics who see this book will not blame me for stating them, but will consider that I could scarcely avoid doing so, as what follows afterwards will be unmixed praise of a Roman Catholic saint. If I am unjust I shall be glad to apologise.

Firstly, I do not consider that the Church of Rome is faithful to truth or to the great eternal difference between right and wrong, and this is the chief reason why I stand apart from it. No Roman Catholic that I have ever yet met forms his opinion on a religious subject by his sense of what is right or wrong, or true or untrue. He only inquires what the Church has decided, and then he argues from that standpoint as well as he knows how. The question is closed for him of whether the Church was right or wrong. There is no possibility of error. A dead wall is between him and freedom of thought, and he glories in the wall. If he doubted, it would crumble to pieces, and it often does crumble to pieces if he fixes his mind and heart only on what is true and right. Then he finds himself free but gasping. Roman Catholicism means an iron slavery of thought, both for individuals and nations. Slaves may be good and happy, but English people do not generally wish to be slaves. For myself, the more I see of Roman Catholics, and the more I love them, the less I wish to become one of them.

Secondly, The Church of Rome, in spite of

plaintive explanations and protestations, does fear the Bible as a cat fears the water. It assures us that it loves the Bible, and has almost created it. It even tells us that we may read it, but it gives us a thousand reasons why it is better for us not to do so, and finally it puts it in its safe and locks it up.

Thirdly, The priests of the Church of Rome are compulsorily celibate. The rule is no doubt a wise one as far as the attainment of worldly power goes. But it is not possible to believe that out of the tens of thousands of young men who in their first youth vow to live celibate lives a majority preserve their purity through all the conflicts of life. And when they fall the whole soul gets crooked, and does crooked work. An unmarried clergyman is a good thing, but he must be free to marry if he should by and by very much wish to marry.

Fourthly, I could not join the Church of Rome because it so little recognises other Christians that a Roman Catholic is actually forbidden even to kneel down and say the Lord's Prayer with a Protestant. This is quite detestable.

Fifthly, The heart's devotion with the great body of Roman Catholics is apparently given to the Virgin Mary and to the Church rather than to the Lord. I say this unwillingly, and I know that there are many exceptions to the rule, but, alas! it is true in the main.

So, God helping me, I will never be a Roman Catholic. And having said this, I feel free to tell my story.

One Sunday morning, in the spring of

1887, I read an account of Father Damien in the magazine of the Soho girls' club, and I made up my mind almost immediately that I would go and see him, and find if there were any way of helping him. The thought of doing so naturally gave me great delight, even though it seemed to me then that visiting Molokai would be the nearest thing to descending into hell.

My plan was to spend the next winter in India, where I had been asked to help in a winter Mission among the native Christians (under the auspices of the Church Missionary Society), and where I was anxious to investigate certain facts as to the prevalence of leprosy, and its possible prevention by some law of segregation. Of the results of this tour in India I hope to speak later, and I would also refer all readers who are willing to acquire further information on this subject to an excellent book by Archdeacon Wright, entitled *Leprosy an Imperial Danger*, which is published by Messrs. Churchill.

After completing my tour in India I took refuge from its terrible heat in Cashmere, where I found more lepers, and where the cholera was raging fearfully. Cashmere is the loveliest country in the world, as far as my experience has gone—a land of snow mountains and rushing rivers, but rich also in noble parklike scenery, where grow the most beautiful trees I ever beheld. The apple and pear orchards were then in such profusion of white and pink blossoms, and the roses, red, white, and yellow, were so delightful, that it seemed as if a universal wedding were going on. The large stars of the white clematis wreathed the trees; all kinds of irises, great and small, abounded; red tulips were to be seen in crowds; and by the glacier's edge grew immense poppies of a gorgeous blue colour. And with all this there was a familiar air about Cashmere. It was like an ideal and glorified England, and I always look back to it as an intimation of

> 'What the world will be,
> When the years have passed away.'

From this paradise a telegram summoned me back to London, and during my somewhat unwilling journey to Bombay I was glad to learn experimentally what the heat is which so many of our countrymen and women endure year after year.

The wind that smote me at the door of the railway carriage was like nothing else but the blast of a furnace, my watch was almost too hot to hold, and the sheets on the bed felt at night as if a warming-pan had just been passed over them. A fellow-passenger told me that in travelling that way some years ago during an exceptionally hot season he had found printed notices in the carriages with directions what to do in case of heat apoplexy, and with particulars of the stations at which coffins could be obtained. Several people died of heat during their journey. Ice was at hand continually, and we sat with towels, in which powdered ice had been folded, round our heads. It was of course a very ordinary experience, so ordinary that little pity is usually spent on it, but one feels proud that one's countrymen are willing to bear so much and to say so little for the sake of ordinary everyday duties. The sea voyage that follows is often worse than the land journey, but we were on this occasion blessed with a headwind and had a prosperous time, and we reached England happily and well.

It is of course not necessary to say anything about my journey across that grayest and most uninteresting of oceans, the Atlantic, or to talk of the Falls of Niagara and the Rocky Mountains. To comfort those who can never see the former I would only remark that the photographs are so excellent that not much is lost by not going to see the original. It is very large, very colourless, and one often remembers how easily it could kill one. But that is a poor sort of thought, and does not generally quicken the pulse. I do not wish, however, to spoil the pleasure of any 'Britisher' as he stands on the soil of Canada gazing at the falls, and rejoices in the proud thought that Queen Victoria owns this beautiful sight! It is certainly well adapted for crowds of travellers to say 'Oh!' at. As to the Rocky Mountains, which some people think so surpassingly beautiful, they are, in my opinion, the ugliest mountains I ever saw, just enormous, disorganised masses of rock, shapeless, bare, and with no idea of how to look like a mountain. Towards the end of the Rio Grande route they certainly become finer, and acquire a grim kind of fairy-tale beauty. Curious pillars and columns and tables stand up on all sides, and the plains between are often rich and beautiful in colour. A soft light yellow grass grows everywhere, with patches of golden or whitish plants. Sometimes the ground is burnt black; sometimes there are the most lovely willow beds, with stems of crimson, purple, and gold. I sketched, but sketching in a very jolting narrow gauge train has its limitations.

I always greatly enjoy the society of Americans who belong to the Eastern States. They are generally delightful, hearty, and witty, and they have a desire to please and a willingness to be pleased which should teach us Englishmen useful lessons. The Bostonians are especially charming, and are highly cultivated in art, music, and in social qualities.

As one gets farther west one finds a notable difference as to good manners, and it must be admitted that the behaviour of the officials at the railway depots is often very bearish.

But there is so much to admire, and the air is so inspiriting, that the traveller generally finds himself in a good humour.

After setting sail from San Francisco we had favouring winds, and our voyage across the Pacific Ocean was full of interest.

Being an artist, I naturally paint a good deal when I am travelling, and I confess that I suffer occasionally from people who kindly come and take an interest in my work.

I was copying Burne Jones's 'Chant d'Amour' one Saturday in the Art Museum at 'Merton' when a polite gentleman came up with a bright-looking boy and said 'My boy is very much interested in seeing you work. Have you any objection to our watching you?' They watched for some considerable time, at the end of which the bright boy said, 'Which is he copying, papa?' My picture was about half-finished. Presently a pleasing young man came up from the art school below, and I civilly asked him if he was working downstairs.

'No,' he said; 'there are no breadcrumbs on Saturdays.'

This mysterious answer staggered me somewhat, but I rallied and asked, 'Do they find you in breadcrumbs, then?'

'Yes; but I wouldn't want a whole loaf, you see, and there are not students enough to divide.'

'I almost wonder you don't bring a roll in your pocket sooner than lose the day.'

'Rolls are too greasy. We want Graham bread.'

(I then became silent, and said to myself—

> 'I would that my tongue could utter
> The thoughts that arise in me.')

Two dirty but agreeable Irishmen came up next, one of whom presently remarked, 'I give you great praise. I am not an artist myself, but I can tell. Any one could hardly say which is the copy' (my canvas was nearly half of it still white). 'Excuse me, friend, but this is not your first picture, is it? Ah! I should say not. Am I a Bostonian? No, I am from the old counthry. I am living with an aunt. I find it pleasant. I have had nothing to do for five weeks.'

A particularly intelligent boy was my next visitor; he stayed a very long time, and even walked back with me to the hotel door.

He began, 'Are you copying? It's pretty exact. It looks a good deal like it. I could easily tell it. You don't use your stool. How many pictures have you copied? Which? . . . If I was doing it, it would be all done now. You have to take drawing lessons first, I suppose? How much shall you sell it for? I don't see how in the world you could make it cost so much. D'you know Mr. Duncan in England? He's the foster-father of one of my friends.'

Another student watched me for two hours, saying that all the places downstairs had been taken, and that he derived great benefit from seeing me paint. He said, ' How funny it seems to snap on the colour that way —rush it on any way. I suppose you think you get a better effect? I am trying lithography. There's a good deal to be got at it if you *could.* If you couldn't, why, there's nothing at all. I've got a friend and he's so disagreeable he can't earn his living. He's disagreeable all round. I think he's real mean.' When I painted the red on the robe of Eros he said, ' Looks as if you had cut your finger over it, doesn't it ? '

Generally people give me an impression of being considerably disappointed in my work—notably one lady did, who belonged to the class of persons who try to look haughty at hotels. Most of the remarks which I am going to record have been made very many times during a sea voyage.

Young man of the dandy kind.—' Painting must be a pleasant way of passing the time, I should suppose?'

Older man.—'Well, I should never have the patience to do it.' (This is a very common observation, implying that the speaker possesses all the requisites except patience, and that he would think twice before choosing work which produced such small results in comparison with the outlay of his valuable time.)

Little girl (*willing to take advice if she is wrong*).—'You have soft colours. I have a paint-box, but I have to scrub my paints.'

Young lady (*a constant attendant*), *for the fifth time.*—' Isn't it wonderful to see it *grow?*

I like to see it *grow*. You don't mind me watching you, do you? because it is as good as a lesson to me. I do so like to see it *grow*.'

Man.—' Looks almost like coloured crayons, doesn't it?'

Impetuous child of thirteen (rushing suddenly to my side).—' Oh my! that's *much better*, isn't it? Don't *you* think it's much better than what you did yesterday?'

Gentleman.—' I suppose when you get home you will work these up into large pictures, won't you?' (This is a very usual thing to say, and means that to the ordinary naked eye there is no excuse for producing such poor results.)

Lady (to comfort me).—' It would be *impossible* to make much of such a subject as that. I am sure no one could do it. You are so good-natured not to mind (!!!) our looking on.'

Aforesaid young lady.—' Oh, can't you see it *growing!* '

Such comments are certainly a little disturbing, but they are all kindly meant, and it would be a shame to complain of them. I look back with pleasure on all the voyages I have ever made, and on nearly all my fellow-passengers.

On the 11th of last December I found myself sailing past the longed-for island of Molokai, and could see the little white buildings of the leper villages, and make sketches of the cloud-capped island, with the rays of light slanting down among its mountains. The weather was deliciously warm and the sea at last was calm. My heart went out to Father Damien.

Hitherto the swell had been enormous, though the surface of the waves was as smooth as oil. We sailed past numbers of nautiluses, which looked like tiny deep-blue dishes with a delicate little transparent sail set up; and following us all the way there were fifteen sooty albatrosses, which fed on the ship's refuse — dark birds with long crooked pinions, and always on the wing.

The coming to Honolulu is very pleasant. The country is beautiful, the hotel is comfortable, and the inhabitants — white and brown — give visitors a hearty welcome.

I received unvarying kindness from every one in the Sandwich Islands, and it is pleasant to find what a high moral and religious tone is established there. The principal people are chiefly the children and grandchildren of the first missionaries, and they have held to the traditions of their fathers.

The leading banker, Mr. C. A. Bishop, married a royal princess, who was a woman of great power and goodness, and their charities have been at once wise and munificent.

There has been some annoyance felt in Honolulu at the sensational and exaggerated accounts which have been written about Hawaiian leprosy, and it is only right to say that visitors need have no fear of contracting this disease, as the Government removes all sources of danger far more efficiently than is done in Europe, Asia, or Africa. In India the opportunities of contracting leprosy are ten times greater than in Hawaii. Visitors are rightly discouraged, and even prevented, from going to the leper settlement, and it was with some difficulty that, owing to the kindness of Dr. Emerson, the President of the Board of Health, I at last obtained permission to visit it for a fortnight, and to take with me a case of gurjun oil in which I was much interested as a remedy. I may mention here that this oil is the produce of a fir-tree which grows plentifully in the Andaman Islands (off the coast of Burmah). Its efficacy was first discovered by Dr. Dougall, and I am assured by Sir Donald Stewart, who was then Governor of the Islands, and who has lent me the official medical report, that every case in the place was cured by it after some months' treatment. The lepers were convicts, and it was therefore possible to enforce four hours a day of rubbing the ointment all over their bodies. They began early in the morning by cleansing their bodies with dry earth, then they rubbed in the oil for two hours, and finally washed it off. They went through the same process in the afternoon, and each time they took a small dose internally. In some of the cases the disease was of many years' standing, and the state to which it had reduced its victims was indescribably dreadful, yet after eight months the sufferers were able to run and to use a heavy pickaxe, and every symptom of leprosy had disappeared. The oil is brown and sticky in its raw condition, but when shaken up with three parts of lime-water it makes an ointment as soft and smooth as butter. It can be obtained in London for eightpence or tenpence a pound through the principal chemists. The internal maximum dose is half an ounce of a mixture of equal quantities of lime-water and oil. The taste is not disagreeable. The real difficulty in the cure lies in the fact that lepers are as a rule too inactive and too callous to take the exertion of sufficient rubbing in of the oil, and it is difficult both in Hawaii and in India to force them to do so. In Molokai there are three Franciscan sisters who take charge of the leper girls, and who are now using the oil. I think that their quiet systematic endeavours are likely to produce important results, and that children will be more obedient patients than adults. I have lately (10th of June) received satisfactory accounts of the state of the lepers who have been using this remedy.

CHAPTER II

HAWAIIANS AND HAWAII

WE English cannot be expected to take great interest in the production of tons and tons of brown sugar, and we shall willingly admit that the things in the Hawaiian Islands which we chiefly care to hear about are, firstly, the leper settlement at Molokai, and secondly, the volcano of Kilauea, the great lake of fire.

The islands lie in the Pacific Ocean, about half-way between America and Australia, and they were discovered a hundred and twenty years ago by Captain Cook. For fifty years they were visited by no white people except merchantmen and whalers, who often exercised on the people a pernicious influence which it makes one's blood boil to hear of. The natives were a fine muscular race, with brown skins and handsome countenances. They were wonderfully hospitable, and they welcomed the first foreigners almost as if they had been gods, giving them freely the best of their food, their shelter, and their daughters. They numbered about four hundred thousand. Their visitors brought them vices—drink and wicked diseases—and now the number of natives has shrunk to forty thousand. Of these it is feared that two thousand are infected with leprosy. Their constitutions are often enfeebled, and their lands are largely held by their guests; but the same hospitable smiles adorn their friendly faces, and the same simple, dignified manners grace their behaviour. They bear no malice.

Happily there is a bright side as well as a dark side to the incoming of the whites.

In the year 1809 a brown boy was found crying on the doorsteps of a college in America. His name was Obookiah, and he came from the Hawaiian Islands. His father and mother had been killed in his presence, and as he was escaping with his baby-brother on his back, the little one was slain with a spear and he himself was taken prisoner. Circumstances brought him to America, and at last to the doorsteps of Yale College. In this extremity he was taken in and kindly used by Mr. Dwight, a resident graduate. Obookiah loved his people, and soon he asked that he might 'learn to read this Bible, and go back home and tell them to pray to God up in heaven.' Two other lads, Tennooe and Hopu, had come to America with him. They were all taken and educated by Mr. Dwight, and the result was that in ten years a band of twelve men and women started from Boston for the Sandwich or Hawaiian Islands, with Tennooe and Hopu as guides. Obookiah had died a peaceful Christian death about a year after his arrival at Yale.

When the party left Boston it was said to them, 'Probably none of you will live to witness the downfall of idolatry.' But when they reached the islands the downfall had already come.

Kamehameha the First—a king as great in his way, perhaps, as our King Alfred—had effected an immense revolution. He had, after long wars, united all the islands in one sovereignty, and he had abolished the degrading system of caste, or 'tabu.' 'By this system' (I quote from Dr. Bartlett's historical sketch of the Hawaiian Mission) 'it was death for a man to let his shadow fall upon a chief, to enter his enclosure, or to stand if his name were mentioned in a song. In these and other ways "men's heads lay at the feet of the king and the chiefs." No woman might eat with her husband, or eat fowl, pork, cocoanut, or bananas—things offered to the idols: death was the penalty.' 'How did you lose your eye?' said Mrs. Thurston, a missionary's wife, to a little girl. 'I ate a banana,' replied the child. If any man made a noise when prayers were being said he died. When the people had finished building a temple some of them were offered in sacrifice. I myself saw a great quadrangular temple, on the coast of Hawaii, which contained quantities and quantities of human skulls. A cord is preserved with which one high priest had strangled twenty-three victims. Infanticide was a common practice. Maniacs were stoned to death. Old people were often buried alive or left to perish. There was no written language.

The missionaries reached Hawaii on the 31st of March 1820, after a long, wearisome journey round South America, and one can imagine how delightful the aspect of these delicious tropical islands must have been to them. The whole scene is so exactly described in the following lines of Tennyson that it seemed to me, when I was there last January, as if they must have been written to describe it—

'Courage!' he said, and pointed toward the land,
'This mounting wave will roll us shoreward soon.'
In the afternoon they came unto a land
In which it seemed always afternoon.
All round the coast the languid air did swoon,
Breathing like one that hath a weary dream.
Full-faced above the valley stood the moon ;
And like a downward smoke, the slender stream
Along the cliff to fall and pause and fall did seem.

A land of streams! some, like a downward smoke,
Slow-dropping veils of thinnest lawn, did go ;
And some thro' wavering lights and shadows broke,
Rolling a slumbrous sheet of foam below.
They saw the gleaming river seaward flow
From the inner land : far off, three mountain-tops,
Three silent pinnacles of aged snow,
Stood sunset-flush'd.

The mountains and the river are there, and the delicious streams are for ever falling by scores down the green precipices of Hawaii into the blue sea. How lovely that sea is can scarcely be told. One puts one's hand in, and all round it is the softest and most brilliant blue; below are growths of pure white coral, and among them swim fishes as brilliant as paroquets. Some are yellow like canaries, some are gorgeous orange or bright red. I tried to paint a blue fish, but no pigment could represent its intensity. The loveliest of all was like nothing but a rainbow as it sported below me. Groves of cocoanut-trees rise from the water's edge. The gardens are rich with roses, lilies, myrtles, gardenia, heliotrope, and passion-flowers.

Near by is a great tropical forest, which I always feared as I entered; for there is an element of the terrible in this tremendous vegetation, and in the perfect silence of it all. The trees are wreathed with humid creepers; the ferns are fourteen feet high; even the stag's-horn moss grows taller than a man. Every foot of space is occupied with rank vegetation.

When the Bostonians reached the coast they sent Hopu on shore to reconnoitre. He soon returned, and as he came within hail he shouted, 'Kamehameha is dead. His son Liholiho reigns. The tabus are abolished. The images are burned. The temples are destroyed. There has been war. Now there is peace!'

This was news indeed. The great king had one day risen up from the place where he was feasting and had stalked over to his wives' table, and sat down with them to eat and to drink. The high priest had followed his example. The people were aghast with apprehension; but no judgment from heaven followed, and soon the tabu was broken everywhere, and a new freedom spread through the islands.

Kamehameha's work was done; he fell ill, and took to his bed. As he lay dying he asked an American trader to tell him about the Americans' God. 'But,' said the native informant, in his broken English, 'he no tell him anything.'

The missionaries had arrived at the right moment, and they were cordially welcomed. The new king, with his five wives, came to call — straight out of the sea, and all undressed. The missionaries hinted that it would be better if they wore clothes, and the next time the king called he wore a pair of silk stockings and a hat. He threw himself down on the bed, the first he had ever beheld, and rolled himself over and over on it with extreme delight.

The Princess Kapuliholiho said to the missionary's wife, 'Give us your eldest son, and we will adopt him.' But the tempting offer was politely declined. There were five dowager-queens, one of whom was dressed with great state in a robe made of seventy thicknesses of bark. The white ladies found favour in the eyes of the brown ladies, who described their visitors in the following terms: 'They are white and have hats with a spout. Their faces are round and far in. Their necks are long. They look well.'

The royal feasts were on a large scale; sometimes as many as two hundred dogs were cooked, and it was a favourite joke to put a pig's head on a roasted dog, to deceive a too fastidious white visitor.

The royal personages and the chiefs claimed the privilege of first learning to read, but the king's intemperate habits made him a somewhat irregular pupil.

A majestic chieftainess, six feet high, named Kapiolani, was one of the first converts to Christianity, and a faithful ally of the teachers of the new faith. It was she who in 1824 broke the spell which hung over the great volcano, the supposed home of the terrible goddess Pele. She marched with her retinue across the plains of lava till she reached the lake of fire. Then she flung into it the sacred ohelo berries, and defied Pele to hurt her. There was a horror-stricken silence, but no calamity followed, and Kapiolani calmly turned to her people and told them of Jehovah and of her new-found faith in Christ.

It is said that a third of the population became Christians in consequence of this brave deed. We who do not believe in Pele may scarcely appreciate the heroism of this action, but the courageous Kapiolani had all the beliefs of her youth to combat, and must have stifled many qualms before she performed her act of defiance.

I have heard an interesting account of the first Sunday school held in Hawaii. The native monitor was found arranging the class into divisions of Christian and non-Christian. He asked every one the question, 'Do you love your enemies?' If they said 'Yes' they were arranged with the Christians, if they said 'No' with the heathen. I have known less sensible divisions made in England; but the missionaries took a broader view, and checked their pupil, much to his surprise.

Only one thing was taught on this occasion to the scholars. They were asked, 'Who made you?' and they were taught to answer, 'The great God, who made heaven and earth.'

It was a simple beginning, but great results soon began to appear. The most intense religious interest was felt all over the islands. Thousands of converts were baptized, a wonderful devotion became apparent, and in a comparatively small number of years the whole population became Christian, and has remained so ever since.

The first band of missionaries were Congregationalists, and to their zeal and godly living is due mainly the praise of changing the religion of the Sandwich Islands from heathenism to Christianity. Their influence is transmitted to their successors, and the services at Fort Street Church and at the native churches are models of simple hearty worship.

The Roman Catholic religion was established there in 1839, and our English Church raised its cathedral later still.

CHAPTER III

FATHER DAMIEN AND MOLOKAI

(Written at Honolulu in last January)

THE little steamer *Mokolii* leaves Honolulu, the capital of the islands, on Mondays at five o'clock for Molokai, and on the 17th of last December I took my passage and went on board.

The sunset was orange, with a great purple cloud fringed with gold. It faded quickly, and by the time we reached a small pier-head outside the town it was dark, and the moon was casting a long greenish light across the sea. From the pier came a continuous tremolo wail, rather mechanical, but broken by real sobs. I could see a little crowd of lepers and lepers' friends waiting there. 'O my husband!' cried a poor woman again and again. Thirteen lepers got into the boat and were rowed to the steamer. Then we sailed away, and gradually the wailing grew fainter and fainter till we could hear it no longer.

These partings for life between the lepers and their families are most tragic, but they are inevitable; for whether the disease be propagated by heredity or by contagion, the necessity for absolute segregation is equally evident, and the Hawaiian Government has risen to the emergency — would that our Indian Government with its probable two hundred and fifty thousand lepers would do likewise!—and, sparing neither labour nor expense, has sought out the cases one by one, and provided a home so suitable to their needs, so well ordered, and so well supplied, that, strange to say, the difficulty often arises of preventing healthy people from taking up their abode there. I know many sadder places than Molokai, with its soft breezes, its towering cliffs, and its sapphire sea. The Hawaiians are a happy, generous people, the fit offspring of these sunny windy islands; they yield themselves up readily to the emotion of the present whether for grief or laughter, and (even with lepers) smiles and play follow close behind tears and sorrow.

The sleeping accommodation on the *Mokolii* is necessarily limited, but being a foreigner, and therefore a passenger of distinction, a mattress was spread for me on the little deck. It was very short, and, moreover, it was soon invaded from the lower end by two pairs of legs—a Chinese pair and a Hawaiian pair. I could not be so inhospitable as to complain of their vicinity, and as a lady kindly enlivened the company by continuous guitar music, accompanied by her own voice and by as many of the passengers as chose to chime in, I relinquished my couch, and, retiring to another part of the vessel, gave myself up to the enjoyment of the moonlit precipices and ravines of Molokai, which we began to coast about midnight. Very solemn and rather terrible they looked.

The island is long, and shaped like a willow-leaf; it lies in the form of a wedge on the Pacific, very low on the south coast, and gradually rising to its greatest altitude, from which the descent—1500 feet—to the northern coast is precipitous. Between the base of these precipices and the sea lie the two leper villages of Kalawao and Kalaupapa. Not improbably half the island is sunk in the sea, and the villages are in the actual cup of the crater of an immense volcano, half of which is submerged.

The Sandwich Islands are a collection of volcanoes of which the fires appear to have died out in southward order. In Hawaii, the largest and most southerly island, they still rage. Out of its great lake of liquid boiling lava the fire-fountains toss themselves high into the air, red as blood in daylight, orange at twilight, and yellow as a primrose by night—a fearful sight, and approached by three miles of scarcely less terrible lava, black and glittering, and hardened into shapes like gigantic crocodiles and serpents.

Sometimes the traveller sees that it is red-hot only eight inches below the sole of his foot.

Even more wonderful, perhaps, is the great extinct crater of Haleakala on the island of Maui. It is the largest crater in the world—nine miles in diameter—and it contains in its hollow fourteen great tumuli or extinct volcanoes, some of them 700 feet high. As I watched the scene at sunrise it seemed to me that I was not only in another planet, but in another dispensation.

Except the crater, there was nothing to be seen around or below me but miles and miles of white clouds, slowly turning pink before the coming sun. Above them arose two far distant mountain-tops, Mona Loa and Mona Kea, and occasionally there was a rent in the great tracts of cloud, and a bit of blue sea appeared.

The vast crater yawned in the immediate foreground, a deathly abandoned place, but not without the beauty which almost always marks Nature's works, if we have but eyes to see them aright. The strange lights and shadows were unlike anything which I have ever beheld before or since. The colours of the tumuli were dim but splendid, going through the range of dull purple, dull pink, dull brown, dull yellow, dull green. The floor of the crater was gray and black, composed of the dust of lava accumulated through centuries, and probably never trodden by the foot of man. Long ago it was a nine miles' expanse of boiling fiery liquid.

As we approached Molokai I found that the slow work of centuries had nearly covered its lava with verdure. At dawn we were opposite Kalaupapa. Two little spired churches, looking precisely alike, caught my eye first, and around them were dotted the white cottages of the lepers, who crowded the pier to meet us. But the sea was too rough for us to land. The coast is wild, and, as the waves dashed against the rocks, the spray rose fifty feet into the air. I never had seen such a splendid surf.

We went on to Kalawao, but were again disappointed; it was too dangerous to disembark. Finally it was decided to put off a boat for a rocky point about a mile and a half distant from the town. Climbing down this point we saw about twenty lepers, and 'There is Father Damien!' said our purser; and, slowly moving along the hillside, I saw a dark figure with a large straw hat. He came rather painfully down, and sat near the water-side, and we exchanged friendly signals across the waves while my baggage was being got out of the hold—a long business, for, owing to the violence of the sea, nothing else was to be put on shore. The captain and the purser were both much interested in my gurjun oil, and they spared no trouble in unshipping it. At last all was ready, and we went swinging across the waves, and finally chose a fit moment for leaping on shore. Father Damien caught me by the hand, and a hearty welcome shone from his kindly face as he helped me up the rock. He immediately called me by my name, 'Edward,' and said it was 'like everything else, a providence,' that he had met me at that irregular landing-place, for he had expected the ship to stop at Kalaupapa, and Father Conradi had gone there. But a leper young lady, who had landed before me in the boat with the other lepers (I had eschewed this boat), had told him that there was a real foreigner on board not merely from America, but from England, and in consequence of her information he had come.

He is now forty-nine years old—a thick-set, strongly-built man, with black curly hair and short beard, turning gray. His countenance must have been handsome, with a full, well-curved mouth and a short, straight nose; but he is now a good deal disfigured by leprosy, though not so badly as to make it anything but a pleasure to look at his bright, sensible face. His forehead is swollen and ridged, the eyebrows are gone, the nose is somewhat sunk, and the ears are greatly enlarged. His hands and face look uneven with a sort of incipient boils, and his body also shows many signs of the disease, but he assured me that he had felt little or no pain since he had tried Dr. Goto's system of hot baths and Japanese medicine. The bathrooms that have been provided by the Government are very nice.

I think he had not much faith in the gurjun oil, but at my request he began using it, and after a fortnight's trial the good effects became evident to all. His face looked greatly better, his sleep became very good instead of very bad (he had only been able to sleep with his mouth open), his hands improved, and last Sunday he told me that he had been able that morning to sing orisons—the first time for months. One is thankful for this relief, even if it should be only temporary; but it is impossible not to fear that after several years' progress the disease has already attacked the lungs or some other vital organ, and that the remedy comes too late.

I had brought with me a large wooden box of presents from English friends, and it had been unshipped with the gurjun oil. It was, however, so large that Father Damien said it would be impossible for his lepers either to land it from the boat or to carry it to Kalawao, and that it must be returned to the steamer and landed on some voyage when the sea was quieter. But I could not give up the pleasure of his enjoyment in its contents, so after some delay it was forced open in the boat, and the things were handed out one by one across the waves. The lepers all came round with their poor marred faces, and the presents were carried home by them and our two selves.

First came an engraving of Mr. Shield's 'Good Shepherd,' from Lady Mount Temple; then a set of large pictures of the Stations of the Cross, from the Hon. Maude Stanley; then a magic-lantern with Scriptural slides; then numbers of coloured prints; and finally an ariston from Lady Caroline Charteris, which would play about forty tunes by simply having its handle turned. Before we had been at the settlement half an hour Father Damien was showing his boys how to use it, and I rarely went through Kalawao afterwards without hearing the ariston active.

There were beautiful silver presents from Lady Grosvenor and Lady Airlie, and several gifts of money. And, most valuable of all, there was a water-colour painting of the Vision of St. Francis by Mr. Burne Jones, sent by the painter. This now hangs in Father Damien's little room.

I did not feel disposed to have my bag carried by a leper, so the walk to Kalawao was a tiring one, up and down hill, through a broad stream, and then along a beach of boulders shaded by great precipices. But the pleasure of gradually discovering that Father Damien was a finer man than I had even expected made it delightful. And about half-way I refreshed myself by a bathe in the foam of the waves, which were too big to allow of a swim, even if the sharks which infest the place had not been a sufficient reason against it. I was impressed by the quiet way in which he sat down and read and prayed while I bathed, retiring at once into that hidden life which was so real to him. When I was ready to walk on with him he was all animation again, and pointed out to me all the objects of interest.

The cliffs of Molokai are in many places almost perpendicular, and rise to a great height from the water's edge. They are generally in shadow, but the sun almost always casts long rays of light through their sundered tops, and I shall ever remember these rays as a distinguishing mark of the leper towns. The sea foam, too, rises up from their bases in a great swirling mist, and makes an enchanting effect in the mornings. Where the slopes are not precipitous the tropical vegetation grows very rank, and not beautiful, I think, to eyes that have learned to love the birch, the gorse, and the heather.

The coarse wild ginger with its handsome spikes of flowers grows everywhere, and the yellow hibiscus (ugliest of trees), and quantities of the Ki-tree, from the root of which is made the intoxicating spirit which has done such a disastrous work among the natives. The ferns are magnificent. Of birds, the most noticeable that I saw were an exquisite little honeybird, with a curved beak and plumage like scarlet velvet; a big yellow owl, which flies about by daylight; a golden plover, which is very plentiful and very nice to eat; and a beautiful long-tailed, snowy-white creature called the bos'un bird, which wheels about the cliff heights. Besides these there are plenty of imported mynahs and sparrows. The curious little apteryx is almost extinct.

As we ascended the hill on which the village is built Father Damien showed me on our left the chicken farm. The lepers are justly proud of it, and before many days I had a fine fowl sent me for dinner, which, after a little natural timidity, I ate with thankfulness.

On arriving at Kalawao we speedily found ourselves inside the half-finished church which is the darling of his heart. How he enjoyed planning the places where the pictures which I had just brought him should be placed! He had incorporated as a transept of the new church the small building which had hitherto been in use. By the side of it he showed me the palm-tree under which he lived for some weeks when he first arrived at the settlement in 1873.

His own little four-roomed house almost joins the church, and here Father Conradi, who lives on the ground-floor, and who is a man of considerable refinement, met us, and ushered us into the tiny refectory where a meal was prepared. Here we found Brother James, a tall powerful-looking Irishman, who pleased me greatly by his simple earnestness, and by the intense affection which he bore to Father Damien.

By Father Damien's desire we sat at a

separate table, as a precaution against infection; but he was close by, and we were all very happy together.

It was hard to disappoint my kind hosts, but I did not feel hungry enough to eat anything, except some biscuits out of a tin; and when on later occasions I had food pressed upon me, I always chose oranges gathered from a tree which grew not far off. After dinner we went up the little flight of steps which led to Father Damien's balcony. This was shaded by a honeysuckle in blossom. A door from it led into his sitting-room—a busy-looking place, with a big map of the world—and inside it another door opened on his bedroom.

Some of my happiest times at Molokai were spent in this little balcony, sketching him and listening to what he said. The lepers often came up to watch my progress, and it was pleasant to see how happy and at home they were. Their poor faces were often swelled and drawn and distorted, with bloodshot goggle eyes; but I felt less horror than I expected at their strange aspect. There were generally several of them playing in the garden below us.

I offered to give a photograph of the picture to his brother in Belgium, but he said perhaps it would be better not to do so, as it might pain him to see how he was disfigured.

He looked mournfully at my work. 'What an ugly face!' he said; 'I did not know the disease had made such progress.' Looking-glasses are not in great request at Molokai!

While I sketched him he often read his breviary. At other times we talked on subjects that interested us both, especially about the work of the Church Army, and sometimes I sang hymns to him—among others, 'Brief life is here our portion,' 'Art thou weary, art thou languid?' and 'Safe home in port.' At such times the expression of his face was particularly sweet and tender.

One day I asked him if he would like to send a message to Cardinal Manning. He said that it was not for such as he to send a message to so great a dignitary, but after a moment's hesitation he added, 'I send my humble respects and thanks.'

I need scarcely say that he gives himself no airs of martyr, saint, or hero—a humbler man I never saw. He smiled modestly and deprecatingly when I gave him the Bishop of Peterborough's message. 'He won't accept the blessing of a heretic bishop, but tell him that he has my prayers, and ask him to give me his.'—'Does he call himself a heretic bishop?' he asked doubtfully, and I had to explain that the bishop had probably used the term playfully.

He asked many affectionate questions about Mr. Hugh Chapman, who had shown him warm friendship and had sent him a large sum of money.

One day he told me about his early history. He was born on the 3d of January 1841 near Louvain in Belgium, where his brother, a priest, still lives. His mother, a deeply religious woman, died about two years ago, and his father twelve years sooner. On his nineteenth birthday his father took him to see his brother, who was then preparing for the priesthood, and he left him there to dine, while he himself went on to the neighbouring town.

F

Young Joseph (this was his baptismal name) decided that here was the opportunity for taking the step which he had long been desiring to take, and when his father came back he told him that he wished to return home no more, and that it would be better thus to miss the pain of farewells. His father consented unwillingly, but, as he was obliged to hurry to the conveyance which was to take him home, there was no time for demur, and they parted at the station. Afterwards, when all was settled, Joseph revisited his home, and received his mother's approval and blessing.

His brother was bent on going to the South Seas for mission work, and all was arranged accordingly; but at the last he was laid low with fever, and, to his bitter disappointment, forbidden to go. The impetuous

Joseph asked him if it would be a consolation for his brother to go instead, and, receiving an affirmative answer, he wrote surreptitiously, offering himself, and begging that he might be sent, though his education was not yet finished. The students were not allowed to send out letters till they had been submitted to the Superior, but Joseph ventured to disobey.

One day, as he sat at his studies, the Superior came in, and said, with a tender reproach, 'Oh, you impatient boy! you have written this letter, and you are to go.'

Joseph jumped up, and ran out, and leaped about like a young colt.

'Is he crazy?' said the other students.

He worked for some years on other islands in the Pacific, but it happened that he was one day in 1873 present at the dedication of a chapel in the island of Maui, when the bishop was lamenting that it was impossible for him to send a missioner to the lepers at Molokai and still less to provide them with a pastor. He had only been able to send them occasional and temporary help. Some young priests had just arrived in Hawaii for Mission work, and Father Damien instantly spoke.

'Monseigneur,' said he, 'here are your new missioners; one of them could take my district, and if you will be kind enough to allow it, I will go to Molokai and labour for the poor lepers whose wretched state of bodily and spiritual misfortune has often made my heart bleed within me.'

His offer was accepted, and that very day, without any farewells, he embarked on a boat that was taking some cattle to the leper settlement.

When he first put his foot on the island he said to himself, 'Now, Joseph, my boy, this is your life-work.'

I did not find one person in the Sandwich Islands who had the least doubt as to leprosy being contagious, though it is possible to be exposed to the disease for years without contracting it. Father Damien told me that he had always expected that he should sooner or later become a leper, though exactly how he caught it he does not know. But it was not likely that he would escape, as he was constantly living in a polluted atmosphere, dressing the sufferers' sores, washing their bodies, visiting their deathbeds, and even digging their graves.

I obtained while I was in the islands a

report he had written of the state of things at Molokai sixteen years ago, and I think it will be interesting to give a portion of it in his own words.

'By special providence of our Divine Lord, who during His public life showed a particular sympathy for the lepers, my way was traced towards Kalawao in May 1873. I was then thirty-three years of age, enjoying a robust good health.

'About eighty of the lepers were in the hospital; the others, with a very few Kokuas (helpers), had taken their abode farther up towards the valley. They had cut down the old pandanus or punhala groves to build their houses, though a great many had nothing but branches of castor-oil trees with which to construct their small shelters. These frail frames were covered with ki leaves or with sugar-cane leaves, the best ones with pili grass. I myself was sheltered during several weeks under the single pandanus-tree which is preserved up to the present in the churchyard. Under such primitive roofs were living pell-mell, without distinction of age or sex, old or new cases, all more or less strangers one to another, those unfortunate outcasts of society. They passed their time with playing cards, hula (native dances), drinking fermented ki-root beer, home-made alcohol, and with the sequels of all this. Their clothes were far from being clean and decent, on account of the scarcity of water, which had to be brought at that time from a great distance. Many a time in fulfilling my priestly duty at their domiciles I have been compelled to run outside to breathe fresh air. To counteract the bad smell I made myself accustomed to the use of tobacco, whereupon the smell of the pipe preserved me somewhat from carrying in my clothes the noxious odour of the lepers. At that time the progress of the disease was fearful, and the rate of mortality very high. The miserable condition of the settlement gave it the name of a living graveyard, which name, I am happy to state, is to-day no longer applicable to our place.'

In 1874 a 'cona' (south) wind blew down most of the lepers' wretched, rotten abodes, and the poor sufferers lay shivering in the wind and rain, with clothes and blankets wet through. In a few days the grass beneath their sleeping-mats began to emit a 'very unpleasant vapour.' 'I at once,' says Father Damien, 'called the attention of our sympathising agent to the fact, and very soon there arrived several schooner-loads of scantling to build solid frames with, and all lepers in distress received, on application, the necessary material for the erection of decent houses.' Friends sent them rough boards and shingles and flooring. Some of the lepers had a little money, and hired carpenters. 'For those without means the priest, with his leper boys, did the work of erecting a good many small houses.'

Since the accession of King Kalakaua the care and generosity of the present Hawaiian Government for their lepers cannot be too highly praised. The Queen and the heir-apparent (Princess Liliuokilani) have visited the settlement in person. The cottages are now neat and convenient, and raised on trestles so as not to be in contact with the earth. There are five churches, and the faces one sees are nearly always happy faces. Each person receives five pounds of fresh beef every week, besides milk, poi, and biscuits. There is a large general shop where tinned fruits and all sorts of things can be bought. Food, no doubt, is somewhat monotonous in quality, and it pleases me to remember how Father Damien enjoyed some raisins I had brought from America as he sat on my balcony.

Of course I saw cases in the hospitals that were terribly emaciated and disfigured, but there is no doubt that the disease has taken a milder form than it wore years ago. As a rule, the lepers do not suffer severe pain, and the average length of life at Molokai is about four years, at the end of which time the disease generally attacks some vital organ. Women are less liable to it than men. One woman accompanied her husband to Molokai when he became a leper, and at his death became the bride of another leper. He died, and she married another, and another after his demise. So that she has lived with four leper husbands, and yet remains healthy.

Dr. Swift, the resident physician, is kind and diligent, and the Government is scrupulous about meeting the wishes of the people in all possible ways.

The children are well cared for in the Kapiolani Home at Honolulu if they show no signs of disease, and those in Molokai certainly do not lead an unhappy life.

They sing very nicely. One man had a full sweet baritone, and there was a tiny child who made a great effect with a bawling metallic voice. A refined-looking woman played the harmonium well, with hands that looked as if they must have been disabled. She had been a well-known musician in Honolulu.

I enjoyed the singing of the Latin Christmas hymn 'Adeste fideles.' But the most touching thing was the leper song (composed by a native poet), a kind of dirge in which they bewailed the misery of their lot. When I visited the boys with Father Damien in the evening they were drawn up in a long narrow lane, which it was rather terrible to inspect by the dim light of oil lamps.

On Sunday evening I showed them the magic-lantern, and Father Damien explained to them the pictures from the life of Christ. It was a moving sight to see the poor death-stricken crowd listening to the story of His healings and then of His sufferings, His crucifixion and His resurrection.

How wonderful is the power of our Saviour to give joy even to lepers. I shall never forget visiting last March an asylum of these poor sufferers at Agra. Their faces were too dreadful to look at; they were lame and maimed and mutilated, but they were singing with husky voices the praises of Jesus Christ, and as I spoke to them of Him they kept repeating the last words of every sentence with the greatest delight, and when I left them the cry rang out again and again, 'Victory to Jesus.' An American Baptist missionary, Mr. Jones, had found time to visit them about once a fortnight with the good news, and here was the result manifested.

In the daytime at Molokai one sees the people sitting chatting at their cottage doors, pounding the taro root, to make it into their favourite food poi, or galloping on their little ponies—men and women alike astride—between the two villages. And one always receives the ready greeting and the readier smile. These changes have been brought about partly by the increased care of the Government itself, and partly by the representations of the noble man who went alone to that plague-stricken place when it was the abode of unmitigated terrors.

It would undoubtedly be a great trial to heart and nerve to live even now at Molokai, as eight noble men and women have elected to do for Christ's sake. I found it distressing during only fourteen days to see none but lepers, and it often came with a specially painful shock to find a child of ten with a face that looked as if it might belong to a man of fifty. But I had gone to

Molokai expecting to find it scarcely less dreadful than hell itself, and the cheerful people, the lovely landscape, and the comparatively painless life were all surprises. I was specially impressed by a good old blind man in the hospital, who told me that he was thankful for the disease, because it had saved him from so much evil.

God's care is surely over all His children, and sooner or later the darkest horrors reveal Divine wisdom and love.

'I learnt by experience,' said a friend of mine to me once, 'that in falling over precipices, in sinking in swamps, in tumbling into pits, in drowning in seas, I did but find God at the bottom—

> 'Thus does Thy hospitable greatness lie
> Outside us like a boundless sea;
> We cannot lose ourselves where all is home,
> Nor drift away from Thee.'

In the early days the state of things must have been very dreadful.

'On my arrival,' says Father Damien, 'I found the lepers in general very destitute of warm clothing. If they have suitable clothes to protect themselves from the inclemency of the weather, they usually resist the cold very well, but they suffer greatly if, through neglect or destitution, they have barely enough to cover their nakedness. They then begin to feel feverish and cough badly, swelling in the face and limbs sets in, and if not speedily attended to the disease generally settles on the lungs, and thus hastens them on the road to an early grave.

'A person afflicted with leprosy who quietly gives himself up to the ravages of the disease, and does not take exercise of any kind, presents a downcast appearance, and threatens soon to become a total wreck.

'I remember well that when I arrived here the poor people were without any medicines, with the exception of a few physics and their own native remedies. It was a common sight to see people going around with fearful ulcers, which, for the want of a few rags or a piece of lint and a little salve, were left exposed. Not only were their sores neglected, but any one getting a fever, or any of the numerous ailments that lepers are heir to, was carried off for want of some simple medicine. . . .

'In the fulfilment of my duties as priest, being in daily contact with the distressed people, I have seen and closely observed the bad effect of forcible separation of the married companions. It gives them an oppression of mind which in many instances is more unbearable than the pains and agonies of the disease itself. This uneasiness of the mind is in course of time partly forgotten by those unfortunates only who throw themselves into a reckless and immoral habit of living. Whereas, if married men or women arrive here in company with their lawful mates, they accept at once their fate with resignation, and very soon make themselves at home in their exile. Not only is the contented mind of the leper secured by the company of his wife, but the enjoyment of good nursing and the assistance so much needed in this protracted and loathsome disease. . . .

'Previous to my arrival here it was acknowledged and spoken of in the public papers as well as in private letters that the greatest want at Kalawao was a spiritual leader. It was owing in a great measure to this want that vice as a general rule existed instead of virtue, and degradation of the lowest type went ahead as a leader of the community. . . . When once the disease prostrated them women and children were often cast out, and had to find some other shelter. Sometimes they were laid behind a stone wall, and left there to die, and at other times a hired hand would carry them to the hospital.

'As there were so many dying people, my priestly duty towards them often gave me the opportunity to visit them at their domiciles, and although my exhortations were especially addressed to the prostrated, often they would fall upon the ears of public sinners, who little by little became conscious of the consequences of their wicked lives, and began to reform, and thus, with the hope in a merciful Saviour, gave up their bad habits.

'Kindness to all, charity to the needy, a sympathising hand to the sufferers and the dying, in conjunction with a solid religious instruction to my listeners, have been my constant means to introduce moral habits among the lepers. I am happy to say that, assisted by the local administration, my labours here, which seemed to be almost in vain at the beginning, have, thanks to a kind Providence, been greatly crowned with success.'

The water supply of Molokai was a pleasant subject with Father Damien. When he first arrived the lepers could only obtain water by carrying it from the gulch on their poor shoulders; they had also to take their clothes to some distance when they required washing, and it was no wonder that they lived in a very dirty state.

He was much exercised about the matter, and one day, to his great joy, he was told that at the end of a valley called Waihanau there was a natural reservoir.

He set out with two white men and some of his boys, and travelled up the valley till he came with delight to a nearly circular basin of most delicious ice-cold water. Its diameter was seventy-two feet by fifty-five, and not far from the bank they found, on sounding, that it was eighteen feet deep. There it lay at the foot of a high cliff, and he was informed by the natives that there had never been a drought in which this basin had dried up. He did not rest till a supply of water-pipes had been sent them, which he and all the able lepers went to work and laid. Henceforth clear sweet water has been available for all who desire to drink, to wash, or to bathe. Lately the water arrangements have been perfected under Government auspices by Mr. Alexander Sproull, who was engaged in this beneficent work while I was at Kalawao, and who was my companion at the guest-house.

Father Damien was not hopeless about the discovery of a cure for leprosy. 'But, to my knowledge, it has not yet been found,' he said. 'Perchance, in the near future, through the untiring perseverance of physicians, a cure may be found.' When newcomers arrived at Molokai there were plenty of old residents ready to preach to them the terrible axiom, 'Aole kanawai ma keia wahi'—'In this place there is no law.' With the greatest indignation Father Damien heard this doctrine proclaimed in public and private, and with the whole force of his being he set himself to combat it.

Along the base of the cliffs there grows very abundantly a plant which the natives call 'ki' (*Dracæna terminalis*), and from the root of which, when cooked and fermented, they make a highly intoxicating liquid. When Father Damien arrived he found that the practice of distilling this horrible drink was carried on largely. The natives who fell under its influence forgot all decency and ran about nude, acting as if they were stark mad. It was illegal to distil spirits, and the brave man, having discovered that certain members of the police were in league with the evil-doers, set to work and went round the settlement with 'threats and persuasions,' till he had induced the culprits to deliver up the utensils which were employed for that purpose. Some of the most guilty persons were convicted, but they were pardoned on giving a promise that they would never offend again. These reforms were of course very unpopular with evil-doers, and there was fierce opposition to his influence. He learnt what it was to be hated for righteousness' sake by the people for whom he was giving his life, and the tide of angry resistance did not entirely turn till it became apparent that the cursed disease had claimed him also for its own. Then his adversaries were ashamed, and became his friends and servants.

It was after living at the leper settlement for about ten years that he began to suspect that he was a leper. The doctors assured him that this was not the case. But he once scalded himself in his foot, and to his horror he felt no pain. Anæsthesia had begun, and soon other fatal signs appeared. One day he asked Dr. Arnim, the great German doctor who was then resident in Molokai, to examine him carefully.

'I cannot bear to tell you,' said Dr. Arnim, 'but what you say is true.'

'It is no shock to me,' said Damien, 'for I have long felt sure of it.'

I may mention here that there are three kinds of leprosy. In one kind the whole body becomes white and of a scaly texture, but the general health is unaffected comparatively. This is the sort repeatedly mentioned in the Bible; in modern times it is somewhat rare.

In the anæsthetic variety the extremities become insensible to pain, and gradually slough away with sores. The whole body becomes weak and crippled, and an easy prey to dysentery or diarrhœa. The third kind of leprosy is named tubercular, and is distinguished by swellings and discolourations. This is the most painful kind to see. Father Damien suffered (as is often the case) both from the anæsthetic and the tubercular forms of the disease.

'Whenever I preach to my people,' he said, 'I do not say "my brethren," as you do, but "we lepers." People pity me and think me unfortunate, but I think myself the happiest of missionaries.'

Henceforth he came under the law of segregation, and journeys to the other parts of the islands were forbidden. But he worked on with the same sturdy, cheerful fortitude, accepting the will of God with gladness, undaunted by the continual reminders of his coming fate which met him in the poor creatures around him.

'I would not be cured,' he said to me, 'if the price of my cure was that I must leave the island and give up my work.'

A lady wrote to him, 'You have given up all earthly things to serve God here and to help others, and I believe you must have *now* joy that nothing can take from you and a great reward hereafter.'—'Tell her,' he said, with a quiet smile, 'that it is true. I *do* have that joy now.'

He was very anxious that I should attend his church services, though, as they were in Hawaiian, I could not understand what was said. English was the language used by educated Hawaiians. He pressed me to help in his choir, and was delighted when I sang 'Adeste fideles' with the boys, and some of the tunes that the ariston played. He had his own private communion in the church on Sunday morning, followed by a general service, at which there were about eighty lepers present.

He seldom talked of himself except in answer to questions, and he had always about him the simplicity of a great man—'clothed with humility.' He was not a sentimental kind of man, and I was therefore the more pleased that he gave me a little card of flowers from Jerusalem, and wrote on it, 'To Edward Clifford, from his leper friend, J. Damien.' He also wrote in my Bible the words, 'I was sick, and ye visited me.' He liked looking at the pictures which were in it, especially at the two praying hands of Albert Dürer and a picture of Broadlands. I told him all the names of the friends who had given me presents for him, and he asked questions, and was evidently touched and happily surprised that English Protestants should love him.

I gave him on Christmas Day a copy of Faber's hymns which had been sent him by Lady Grosvenor's three children. He read over the childishly written words on the title-page, 'Blessed are the merciful, for they shall obtain mercy,' and said very sweetly that he should read and value the book. He was notably fond of children, and solicitous about three little girls who had been removed to Honolulu.

I wished I could have understood the

sermon he preached on Christmas Day. It was long and animated. In the afternoon he was catechising the boys, and he translated for me some of his questions and some of their answers, chiefly bearing on the Nativity and on the nature of God.

In speaking to me he used English, which he said was now the language most natural to him.

It has been generally said in England that he is a Jesuit, but this is not the case. He belongs to the 'Society of the Sacred Heart of Jesus and Mary.'

He was, of course, desirous that the English friends whose sympathy and affection have helped him should belong to his Church, but I was glad to find in conversation with him that it was no part of his belief that Protestants must be eternally lost. He and Father Conradi talked much to me of the infallible authority of the Church, and I felt that if that one dogma could be swallowed, nothing else need surely be refused. There is something attractive about submission to authority, but it has its disastrous side if the authority be only human. Probably the world would have been spared the shame and horror of the fires of Smithfield and the racks of the Inquisition if the great lay body of temperate men and kindly women had felt that they could form a public opinion against ecclesiastical authority. But they dared not assert themselves, and the ghastliest crimes that have disgraced humanity were perpetrated under the name of religion.

The same demon who inspired them has often found a resting-place in Protestant churches, and we remember them not for the sake of reproaching after long years the Church which committed them, but rather to point out the danger of investing even the most religious leaders of the time with irresponsible power. They were, as a great writer has told us, but 'the legitimate fruit of the superstition that in the eyes of the Maker of the world an error of belief is the greatest of crimes; that while for all other sins there is forgiveness, a mistake in the intellectual intricacies of speculative opinion will be punished not with the brief agony of a painful death, but with tortures to which there will be no end.' There is something peculiarly repulsive to the English mind in the faults which are developed from the love of priestly power.

Assent is probably a different thing from conviction, but I tried to explain to Father

Damien that we in England have not the power in us to believe that the Roman Church has made no mistakes in her beliefs, any more than that she has committed no faults in her practice.

He spoke of the comfort it gave him to know that all his fellow-priests preached precisely the same doctrine that he preached, but I could only reply that we would rather have a growing faith on which fresh light can be cast, and from which old abuses can be detached, than a system of doctrine which has been defined at every point for centuries. We do not regard as a desideratum the routine which comes of strict orthodoxy, and we owe much of the force of our spiritual life to the fact that men who have held strongly the primary beliefs as to the difference between right and wrong, the goodness and love of the Almighty Father, and His manifestation in Jesus Christ, have freely searched for truth with no haunting fear that they must not differ from other good men who have gone before them. We are content to believe that perfection of creed grows with perfection of practice.

But, notwithstanding such differences, no sincere man could feel a real barrier in intercourse with one so good as Father Damien, and on his side he always showed a true and wholesome charity while he dealt with views which he considered erroneous.

We must all rejoice that the Roman Catholic Church produces such saints, and not hesitate to accord them the fellowship, the sympathy, and the hearty honest praise which they deserve. To Father Damien we render more than praise. He has our love.

He told me that there had been beautiful instances of true devotion among the lepers. Roman Catholics were nearly as numerous as Protestants, and both Churches were well filled. He gave me good accounts of the Protestant native minister, who had come to Molokai in charge of his leprous wife. I visited him, but we could only understand each other through an interpreter. The total number of lepers in the settlement was a thousand and thirty.

Christmas Day was, of course, a feast, and in the evening the lepers had an entertainment and acted little scenes in their biggest hall. The ariston played its best between whiles. To English people it would probably have seemed a dreary entertainment, but the excitement was great. Belshazzar's feast was a truly wonderful representation, and not much more like Belshazzar's feast than like most other scenes. The stage was very dark, and all the lepers seemed to take their turns in walking on and off it. Belshazzar had his face down on the table, buried in his arms, nearly all the time, and it really seemed as if he might be asleep. Nobody did anything particular, and it was difficult to say who was intended for Daniel. I think the queen-mother was a little boy.

The fathers were on very affectionate, playful terms with the lepers. I found Father Conradi one morning making a list of the boys' names, which I think are worth recording with some others that I got from Mr. Sproull and Dr. Nicholls. It must be remembered that they are boys' names: Jane Peter, Henry Ann, Sit-in-the-cold,

The Rat-eater, The Eyes-of-the-fire, A Fall-from-a-horse, Mrs. Tompkins, The Heaven-has-been-talking, Susan, The Window, The wandering Ghost, The first Nose, The tenth Heaven, The Dead-house, The white Bird, The Bird-of-water, The River-of-truth, The Emetic.

The following names were found by Dr. Nicholls at Honolulu: Mr. Scissors, Mrs. Oyster, The Fool, The Man who washes his Dimples, The tired Lizard, The Atlantic Ocean, The Stomach, The great Kettle, Poor Pussy, The Pigsty.

Father Damien would never come inside the guest-house where I was staying, but sat in the evening on the steps of the verandah and talked on in his cheery, pleasant, simple way. The stars shone over his head, and all the valleys glimmered in golden moonlight. There is often wild weather in Molokai. The cona wind rushes up from the southern coast, and reaches with steady force the heights of the island; then it seems staggered at finding the ground suddenly come to an end, and descends through the gorges to the leper villages in gusts which, though warm, are so violent that one evening our roof was mainly torn off, and the rain came pouring through a dozen fissures. The china-roses by the balcony were ruthlessly withered and torn to pieces, and in a ride from Kalaupapa I was driven in exactly opposite directions within a distance of two hundred yards, while the rain in my face felt more like gravel than water. This weather sometimes lasts for days together, and the wind continues, though the skies may be full of starlight or sunshine.

Generally the climate is what would universally be described as lovely; but Mr. Sproull told me that the heat and stillness were sometimes so exhausting that every one got 'as limp as a wet collar.'

The ground at Molokai is strewn with great black blocks of lava, round which grows a tall delicate grass so closely that one has to be careful of pitfalls as one walks. There are not many wild-flowers in the Sandwich Islands. The lilac major convolvulus, a handsome white poppy, the diverse-coloured lantana, and a bright orange-blossom with a milky stem are among the principal. On the hills grow the crimson-blossomed Lehua, and various pretty berries, white, black, purple, yellow, and red—some of them (the ohelo especially) excellent to eat.

Half-way between the two leper towns

rises a lowish hill, which is found, on ascending it, to be an extinct volcano with a perfect cup, and at the bottom of the cup a hole 130 feet wide which is said to be unfathomable. It is nearly full of turbid green water. Half skeleton trees grow on its sides, and some big cactuses. The place looks like the scene of some weird fairy tale.

At Kalaupapa there live and work Father Wendolen and three Franciscan sisters. Mother Marianne, the Superior, is a very gentle sweet woman with considerable organising powers, and a taste for art and beauty which can find little scope in that outcast place. She told me that she would be glad to receive clothes for the children occasionally. They may be sent direct to her or to the care of the Board of

Health for the leper settlement at Kalaupapa, Molokai, Hawaiian Islands. The Roman Catholic Church in this village was built partly by Father Damien's own hands. He is good at carpentering and building, and apparently able and ready to work at anything as long as it *is* work. He is specially scrupulous and businesslike about accounts and money matters, and was very anxious that I should see how carefully he had kept his books, and that I should understand that the presents sent him had been dispensed with impartiality among Protestants and Roman Catholics. Besides Father Conradi he has with him two earnest laymen —Brother Joseph, an American, and Brother James, an Irishman.

The time for me to leave the leper settlement came only too soon. On the last day of the year a ship came, bringing two hundred friends of lepers to spend a few hours at Molokai—a treat generously provided by Mr. Samuel Damon of Honolulu. The sea was so rough that only the men were allowed to land, but the women were taken close to the shore in boats, so that they could see their friends and converse with them. One bold girl leaped on shore in defiance of all rules. The scenes of meeting and parting were never to be forgotten. When the vessel sailed away all the population seemed to have come out to say farewell, and there was much wailing and waving of handkerchiefs. But what a difference it must make to the sufferers and to their relatives to look forward to such occasional meetings instead of to an unbroken separation!

As our ship weighed anchor the sombre

purple cliffs were crowned with white clouds. Down their sides leaped the cataracts. The little village, with its three churches and its white cottages, lay at their bases. Father Damien stood with his people on the rocks till we slowly passed from their sight. The sun was getting low in the heavens, the beams of light were slanting down the mountain sides, and then I saw the last of Molokai in a golden veil of mist.

* * * * *
* * * * *

LONDON, *May* 1889.

And now the news of Father Damien's death has come to us. Friends have said to me, 'You must be glad to think that he has passed away to his reward.' I feel that all that God does is best, and that therefore this is best. But I do not feel glad except from that highest point of view. Looked at with human eyes, it would have seemed to most of us that so useful and happy a life might have been prolonged with great blessing to himself and to the suffering ones among whom he worked.

I think that in the last few weeks he had himself begun to feel the desires for paradise quickening, as the weariness of the flesh grew heavier.

On the 4th of last January Brother James wrote to me : '. . . Let us all pray that although we may not meet again on earth we shall one day be happily united for ever in our heavenly Father's mansions, where the lepers are clean. I cannot express to you, Mr. Clifford, how highly we have appreciated your visit to our poor leper settlement, nor the delight with which the leper boys hailed each time your presence among them. And they will never forget your generous and successful efforts in promoting their enjoyment. Especially they are delighted to know that you brought from the uttermost parts of the earth a cure for their leprosy. I sometimes offend Father Damien's modesty by telling him he is appearing younger and better looking since using the oil, and really his face and voice have greatly improved. He is having great confidence in its use. He most affectionately thanks your kind inquiry after his health, and wishes you to know that he is improving in every respect.

'He is greatly elated over the good news received from Rev. Mr. Chapman, and requests that when you write home you will express his unbounded gratitude to that zealous friend of the lepers, and all others associated with him in the good work. The reward will be the prayers of the leper priest and his afflicted flock ascending daily to the throne of mercy for all our benefactors. Wishing you all happiness in this life and the next, I remain yours truly in Christ.'

(Father Damien adds a postscript.)

'Being very busy, I endorse all what Brother James says. *Au revoir.* The Lord bless you.　　　　　　　　J. DAMIEN.'

The hopes which this account and my last days at Molokai raised were dashed by a letter from Brother James, written on the 21st of February. He gave a distressing account of Father Damien's bodily condition, but said: 'Nevertheless he is as energetic as ever in bettering the condition of the lepers; there have been added to our number since you left about a dozen new cases; all are comparatively happy.'

The postscript to this letter is—

'My love and good wishes to good friend Edward. I try to make slowly my way of the Cross, and hope to be soon on top of my Golgotha.—Yours for ever,

'J. DAMIEN.'

My last letter from him is dated 28th February:—

'KALAWAO, 28*th February* 1889.

'MY DEAR EDWARD CLIFFORD—Your sympathising letter of 24th gives me some relief in my rather distressed condition. I try my best to carry without much complaining and in a practical way, for my poor soul's sanctification, the long foreseen miseries of the disease, which, after all, is a providential agent to detach the heart from all earthly affection, and prompts much the desire of a Christian soul to be united—the sooner the better—with Him who is her only life.

'During your long travelling road homewards please do not forget the narrow road. We both have to walk carefully, so as to meet together at the home of our common and eternal Father. My kind regards and prayers and good wishes for all sympathising friends. *Bon voyage, mon cher ami, et au revoir au ceil.—Votus tuus,*

'J. DAMIEN.'

About three weeks after writing this letter he felt sure that his end was near, and on the 28th March he took to his bed.

'You see my hands,' he said. 'All the wounds are healing and the crust is becoming black. You know that is a sign of death. Look at my eyes too. I have seen so many lepers die that I cannot be mistaken. Death is not far off.

'I should have liked to see the Bishop again, but *le bon Dieu* is calling me to keep Easter with Himself. God be blessed!

'How good He is to have preserved me long enough to have two priests by my side at my last moments, and also to have the good Sisters of Charity at the *Léproserie*. That has been my *Nunc Dimittis*. The work of the lepers is assured, and I am no longer necessary, and so will go up yonder.'

Father Wendolen said, 'When you are up above, father, you will not forget those you leave orphans behind you?'

'Oh no! If I have any credit with God I will intercede for all in the *Léproserie*.'

'And will you, like Elijah, leave me your

mantle, my father, in order that I may have your great heart?'

'Why, what would you do with it?' said the dying martyr; 'it is full of leprosy.'

He rallied for a little while after this, and his watchers even had a little hope that his days might be lengthened. Father Conradi, Father Wendolen, and Brother Joseph were much in his company. Brother James was his constant nurse. The Sisters from Kalaupapa visited him often, and it is good to think that the sweet placid face and gentle voice of the Mother were near him in his last days. Everybody admired his wonderful patience. He who had been so ardent, so strong, and so playful, was now powerless on his couch. He lay on the ground on a wretched mattress like the poorest leper. They had the greatest difficulty in getting him to accept a bed. 'And how poorly off he was; he who had spent so much money to relieve the lepers had so forgotten himself that he had none of the comforts and scarcely the necessaries of life.' Sometimes he suffered intensely; sometimes he was partly unconscious. The terrible disease had concentrated itself in his mouth and throat. As he lay there in his tiny domicile, with the roar of the sea getting fainter to his poor diseased ears, and the kind face of Brother James becoming gradually indistinct before his failing eyes, did the thought come to him that after all his work was poor, and his life half a failure? Many whom he had hoped much of had disappointed him. Enemies had lurked near at hand. His motives had been impugned, his character had been assailed. Not much praise had reached him.

The tide of affection and sympathy from England had cheered him, but England was so far off that it seemed almost like sympathy and affection from a star. Churches were built, schools and hospitals were in working order, but there was still much to be done. He was only forty-nine, and he was dying.

'Well! God's will be done. He knows best. My work, with all its faults and failures, is in His hands, and before Easter I shall see my Saviour.'

The breathing grew more laboured, the leprous eyes were clouded, the once stalwart frame was fast becoming rigid. The sound of the passing bell was heard, and the wail of the wretched lepers pierced the air. . . . The last flickering breath was breathed, and the soul of Joseph Damien de Veuster arose like a lark to God.

Surely his power on earth now is greater than it ever was while he lived among us! As Christ's power was greater when He was nailed powerless to the Cross by hands and feet than when He went about to heal and bless, and greater still when He rose to heavenly places, so it is with His true servants.

I think that Father Damien is now receiving ten cities as a reward for his careful and diligent use of the 'pound' which he thirty years ago consecrated to God when he presented his body a living sacrifice holy and acceptable for His service. His life and death have power to touch thousands of souls whom he never heard of, power too to make a great nation rise to free an empire from the plague which slew him. What a reward!

Brother James wrote me as follows three days after his death:—

'With heart-felt sorrow I announce to you the death of our friend Father Damien, who departed this life 15th April, having been confined to his bed for twenty-one days, during which time he often suffered intensely, the disease having concentrated itself in his mouth and throat, thus ending a martyrdom of sixteen years.

'I enjoyed the happy privilege of being his sick-nurse, and I was with him night and day until he breathed forth his soul to God in my arms. A happier death I never saw. He was constantly united to God by incessant prayer and suffering; he often told me he was so happy at the hope that he would celebrate the coming Easter in heaven. Yourself and Mr. Chapman were always in his thoughts, as his most devoted friends. A remarkable change in his countenance took place before his death, that of the total disappearance of the tubercles with which his face was covered. We have laid him to rest under his puhalla-tree, almost at the door of my little cottage, where I will act as guardian of the dear remains until I too shall end my course.'

Damien is now called to join that mystical body of Christ which is the 'blessed company of all faithful people,' and I think it will surprise him little when among them he meets men and women of other Christian bodies than that to which he belonged, who have given their lives, as he has done, to the leprous, the foul, and the evil. All were filled with the same divine life; all were inspired with the love and the faith of God ; all are counted worthy to walk in robes of white. Differences of creed separate us pitifully here, but some day we shall perhaps find that the Church's dictum, 'Quod semper, quod ubique, quod ab omnibus,' is true in a deeper and broader sense than that in which she has generally used it, and that a great family is ours of too long unrecognised brothers and sisters.

Surely the bond of union which all kinds of men and women have felt with Father Damien ought to make us realise how much there is of our religion that does not depend on minor differences of creed. When we remember, too, how little of our Bible the Old Testament saints possessed, we must admit that much of the essence of religion is not exclusively drawn from the Bible, though in consideration for our dulness it is set forth in its pages.

St. Paul tells us how adequate for salvation

was the law written in the heart by nature, and nowadays, when so much that is traditional is shaken, and when men are so ready to take refuge from right doing in scepticism, it is time to ask whether beliefs that seem to unbelievers arbitrary beliefs are the only important and inspiring part of Christianity, and whether the law by which they will finally be judged is obligatory, for the reason that it is as natural a part of them as their eyes, their ears, and their breathing. Is there not a universal truth ('Quod semper, quod ubique, quod ab omnibus') which is the heritage of all humanity? And if that truth is neglected or abandoned, is it not from wilful blindness rather than from unwilling scepticism? Are there not some 'things which cannot be shaken'? Is there not 'a kingdom which cannot be moved'?

If we grant this let it be remembered that by doing so we give up no part of our own faith, and that the life of obedience to our risen Lord is to be lived with greater rather than less carefulness. But we have gained vital touch with many who come from the east and the west, from the north and the south, and who have hitherto been regarded by us too much as strangers and foreigners. And we have won a power of invitation to many whom we had hitherto looked at in silence.

Father Damien was a strict and conscientious Roman Catholic, and doubtless assented to all the dogmas of his Church. But all who share the common Christ life feel a sense of brotherhood with him, even if they do not think that the Roman Church is infallible, or that its miracles are all authentic.

And this brotherhood depends surely on truths that are universal, on faithfulness to the great eternal difference between right and wrong, on belief in God as the Spirit who is our Almighty Father—invisible, timeless, omnipresent, triumphant—as the One who truly is Love, Light, and Life, and who has manifested Himself to us in Christ for our salvation.

Let us develop this thought a little further while the lessons of Father Damien's life are fresh in our hearts and minds.

All that is admirable is surely a manifestation of God, and therefore in loving good we love God or what is of God. Peace and rest come to all faithful hearts when they fearlessly recognise and worship God as perfect goodness, when they have at last learnt that 'whatsoever things are true, honest, just, pure, lovely, and of good report,' *just mean God*. The best hopes and the best thoughts are always the truest and the most divine. God's children discard only evil things from their thought of Him, and they even do not complain that He has allowed evil to exist. For while they hate it and fight it they yet know that the work of its destruction is the very means by which they attain to God's thought of them. Without pain and evil and conflict it would surely have been impossible for the highest virtues to have been called into existence.

Is it a part of this universal truth that Christ is the Son of God—that Christ is our Saviour? Is it reasonable to believe that the invisible Spirit should become visible, that God, who is responsible for material things, should manifest Himself as material?

I think it is both natural and reasonable to believe it. And I believe that many doubt it only because they associate false beliefs with this truth. God is our Father and Creator, and as such He must meet every claim that the child and the creature have on Him. But He is a Spirit, and we are material. How then can He manage to be reached and touched by us?

I heard it well said once by Hannah Whitall Smith that if a man desired to make a reform in an ant-hill it would be of no use for him to stand and harangue the ants. He would have to give it up unless he could pass into the body of an ant and become one of them. Then he could make himself understood and effect his purpose.

This is what God has done for us by His incarnation in Christ, and in a lesser degree by His manifestation in all good men and women, and in all nature.

This is what the old world religions have strained after, for men have always considered that the God who made them would surely want to be seen and known by them. Krishna, Osiris, Zeus, Buddha are all proofs of the naturalness of the idea of incarnation. So it was not strange that when the fulness of the time was come God became manifest in the flesh, and showed Himself to us more clearly than He had ever done before.

More than this, He not only showed Himself, but He made it possible for us so to receive Him that in union with the Son of God we should become one with Himself in a more perfect way than our creation involved.

Forgiveness, access, sonship, and absolute

union are given to us; we are called to be 'the fulness of Him Who filleth all in all.' No wonder at the enthusiasm of those who, having received Christ, rejoice in Him as God manifest in the flesh, the image of the invisible God, as the One who opens to them such an experience.

Doubtless, the time will come when we shall see more clearly than we do now how from the beginning Christ was in the world, though the world knew Him not. Wherever God has manifested Himself to men, and wherever they have reached Him, in whom they live and move and have their being, it has been by Christ, though for centuries the name of Jesus was not known.

This identification of God with humanity by Christ is surely a natural and probable thing for our faithful Creator to effect. In

Christ God is afflicted in all our afflictions, He suffers pain and death with us. And thereby He rights us till we reach His own perfect desire for us.

As I sailed to Molokai I learnt something of this truth from the sea. I often leaned over the ship's side and looked at it gleaming in sapphire and emerald, and then turning to whitest, loveliest foam as the keel cleft it.

I saw how all the filth and garbage of the ship were flung into it, and how it received them and absorbed them and yet remained pure. All the refuse of rejected food was poured into it; all the dirty water and foulness of that ship and of all ships; all the dead bodies of its sea-monsters had found their tomb in it, and all the dead bodies of all drowned men and women. Yet it was sweet and clean and clear. Into it the deadliest poison might be poured, and yet none would fear to bathe in it or drink of it the next minute.

So it is with the Christ of God. Though in His divine love He has identified Himself with all wretched sinners, yet He remains spotlessly holy. Though He has borne all the sin of the world, yet it is as nothing. All evil is nullified as it touches Him, and the poor souls who brought it stand pure and clean in Him.

No statement is too strong for the Bible to make as to this identification of the Lord with man. And we shall find that the depths of our own hearts testify to the same truth.

> To one the deepest doctrines seem
>   So naturally true,
> That when he learns the lesson first
>   He scarcely thinks them new.

Perhaps the acceptance of the great principles of our faith may not be so difficult as is sometimes supposed, even for those who, unlike ourselves, are tormented with doubts as to the truth of some of the facts which the Bible records.

They *are* facts, but if they were only divine thoughts would they be less true? Is the story of the Prodigal Son less real because it probably did not actually happen? Should a man refuse to live by the rule of the Bible because it cannot be mathematically proved that it records nothing but literal occurrences? Are not thoughts the realities of facts? Is not faith the substance of things hoped for? Does not everything from a statue to a shoe-buckle exist first as the thought of the creator and then become visible? Its transitory existence in matter depends only on its real existence in thought. And is not the divine thought in a miracle told to us in the Bible a real and inspiring part of it? The actual facts were transitory, the thought is eternal, and is the part that moves us.

The Christian who lives his life by the power of His risen Lord has better proof of his faith than Paley's evidences can give him. Christ has promised that if a man do His works he shall know of the doctrine. Let him then live nobly and divinely, and allow no scepticism to paralyse his work. The greatest religious truth is the truth which 'cannot be shaken,' and the kingdom of God is 'the kingdom which cannot be moved.' Let him go happily to the work of life with the faith and the hope of God, with the indwelling life of

Christ, and with the charity which never faileth.

And so, blessed by the lessons of his life and death, we bid farewell to Father Damien.

All that is mortal of him lies in the little graveyard by the blue sea, where one by one his beloved flock have been laid. The long sad wail of the lepers has been heard day after day for their friend, and many hearts are sore.

The strong, active figure and the cheery voice are no longer to be found at Molokai. God's will be done.

> Fear no more the heat of the sun,
>   Nor the furious winter rages,
> Thou thy worldly task hast done,
>   Home art gone and ta'en thy wages.

CHAPTER IV

THE LAKE OF FIRE

THE volcano of Kilauea is so connected with the former religion of the Sandwich Islands, and is, moreover, so interesting a phenomenon, that a short account of it must find place in this little book.

After my return from Molokai I started from Honolulu as soon as possible for the island of Hawaii, and in about thirty-six hours I found myself landed on its coast, at the little village of Punaluu, where I was hospitably received at the inn by Mr. and Mrs. Lee. It was Saturday night, and the comforts of a bedroom were very welcome after a somewhat stormy voyage. Next morning I rose refreshed to spend a very quiet and happy Sunday.

The time for the little native service at the church was half-past ten. Bells began ringing, but I delayed, thinking that, as I could not understand the language, it would be best to go only for the last part of the service. So I set out about eleven. When I got to church I was the only person there — so leisurely and late are the Hawaiians. By and by came in some tall, giggling school-girls, then three women with a baby, then three men and the minister. At last we were nineteen, and the service proceeded.

The women look just pleasant, good-natured creations, handsome, large, fat, with a ready smile; they have beautiful curving mouths, but cheap, unfinished eyes. They lolled freely, and did not feign more attention to the service than they felt. (This was, as it were, only a small country out-station. In Honolulu I found a large attendance of natives at church, and a keen interest and devout behaviour.) The manners of both men and women are simple and fine, and the dress of the women is picturesque—a long flowing robe made like a dressing-gown. It looks best in black, but I met a tall beautiful girl at Kilauea who wore a dark blue gown, and pink roses in her coils of black hair. Her face was of the Rossetti type, her manners were frank, dignified, and charming, and she sang and danced even before breakfast. The Hawaiians are all passionately fond of flowers, and I saw old women of ninety with large wreaths of blue blossoms and green leaves above their withered faces.

These islanders take no thought for to-morrow and very little for to-day. 'Why should we bother? What does it matter?' Mr. Sproull told me that a Hawaiian did not much mind even having something deducted from his pay when he shirked his work; for he felt no poorer when threatened with the deduction, and when pay-day came he got a good bit of money at any rate and felt rich. There is, however, one thing which a native *does* hate, and that is to be laughed at.

Their ways are very unlike ours. For instance, a white man wishes to buy a horse, but its owner entirely refuses to sell it till a day comes when he wants some money, perhaps for his child's birthday feast. Then he accepts the price offered, and it is agreed that he is to bring the horse in a week and be paid. But in two days the native comes back and says he cannot sell it, because his mother-in-law cried and did not want it to go. At a later stage he again agrees to sell, but after all the white man does not get the horse, for when the seller reaches home another buyer comes in and offers to pay down half the price that had been promised, and the money is taken and the horse is gone away with its new owner. And it is no use to grumble.

Nearly all the natives make speeches, but with little matter in them, and full of negatives. 'What do I say of Queen Pikiliki? That she is a tall woman, with red hair and tusks? No. Do I say that she has only one leg? No.' And so on indefinitely. With all their weaknesses, however, I think that Hawaiians are the most charming natives I ever saw.

On Monday morning I rode up to Kilauea. All down the mountain side lie coils of hardened lava, sometimes grown over with vegetation and sometimes with enormous cracks and rents. Two years ago there was a terrific earthquake in this place, and the lava flowed down to the sea in a river. My host, Mr. Lee, told me that his house rocked like a rocking-chair, and that everything was upset. The ground seemed hollow, and a hissing and whizzing kept going on underneath. There were twenty-five shocks in two hours, and they continued all through the night at intervals.

Three lady visitors, who had the day before been elated with their unusually brilliant experiences at the volcano, were now in abject terror, and sat screaming on the balcony-steps in their night-gowns for two whole hours. They even refused coffee. No lives were lost, however. The sea made a harmless bed for the lava.

It is a long, slow ride up the mountain, but when one reaches the highest elevation the view is sufficiently surprising. The traveller finds himself on a curious green plain, from which many tufts of white smoke are rising. It looks as if weeds were being burned—but no, it is the steam coming out of cracks in the ground, and when he goes up to the place he finds it both hot and wet, and crowds of lucky ferns grow there as thickly as possible. In the middle of this plain is sunk the crater of Kilauea, a monstrous cup, of which the bottom is a waste of lava, and the sides are precipices about nine miles in circumference. In its centre is a small black burning mountain with several peaks, from which volumes of white smoke continually ascend. Nearly at the foot of this mountain the lake of fire is situated. By night the smoke is illuminated, and about a dozen fiery furnaces are seen.

On one side of the crater there is a zigzag path down the precipice, which is clothed with tropical vegetation. The ferns and mosses are beautiful, and everywhere grow the scarlet and yellow ohelo berries, which are in season each month of the year, and which taste something like whortle-berries. They were held sacred to the goddess Pele.

At the bottom of the precipice the vegetation ceases suddenly, and the most absolutely abandoned place is reached. What looked a flat plain from the top is now discovered to be a wilderness of dark lava, all solid, but in every conceivable form of mud wave and mud flow; often it is twisted into coils exactly like rope, and there are regions where it seems as if some intelligence had been at work to shape it into tens of thousands of huge crocodiles and serpents and antediluvian beasts. These wonders must be seen to be believed in. They often look positively wicked. In some parts the sulphur has its way, and the lava erections are bright lemon colour. One place is like a ruined tower, with a red-hot oven half-way up it, and a perpetual squilching and hissing and fizzing going on. Generally the lava is blackish gray in colour; sometimes it is iridescent, sometimes it has a sheen, like satin, and glitters brightly in the sun.

A great deal of it is as hard as stone, but sometimes it is brittle, and is spread out in thin folds like drapery. Under a man's weight it breaks with a scrunch, and down he goes—perhaps for five inches, perhaps for five feet. It is best to follow closely in the guide's footsteps. There are three miles to be walked over before one reaches the mountain. The lava is often rent with wide, deep cracks, and in some places I found that it was red-hot only eight inches below the sole of my foot. Sometimes the crust has heaved and broken; under it is a hollow, and then more lava underneath. The ground is often almost burning hot. Somehow it is not as horrible as one would expect—the sun is so brilliant, the air is so good, and the guide is so cool.

At last the traveller begins to ascend the

spur of the mountain, a very big dreadful crack has to be jumped across, and almost immediately afterwards he looks down, and just below him he sees close at hand the lake of fire. And if he is not frightened and silly he climbs down and stands at its edge, shading his face and eyes from the burning heat, and near enough to dip his long alpenstock into the lava. The lake is about 100 yards in diameter. Its rim rises about ten feet from the ground, and sometimes the boiling lava surges up till it overflows. But the best effects are when the inside wall shows itself for about twelve feet, for then the lava dashes up round it in waves, and continually undermines it with red-hot grottoes till it topples in with a crash. These waves of lava are not unlike the waves of the sea, only their colour is the colour of coral or of blood, and their spray is red instead of white. Above them there is often a beautiful lilac or violet effect, and this violet atmosphere of the lake of fire is one of the loveliest things about it.

The lava is as liquid as thick soup, and of a bluish gray colour, with occasional greenish tints. It keeps simmering and heaving, and then it breaks in all directions into most lovely vermilion cracks, changing into violet and then into dead gray. All the time a roaring sound goes on like the roaring of the sea. Wherever the slightly cooling crust cracks it is red-hot.

And now, as one watches, a scarlet fountain begins to play in the middle of the lake. At first it is about two feet high, with golden spray, then it gets wilder and larger and more tumultuous, tossing itself up into the air with a beautiful sportiveness—great twistings of fiery liquid spring into the air, like serpents and griffins. It is terrible. It is splendid. It is exquisite. And it is almost indescribable. I visited the volcano six times, and generally saw some of these fire fountains, and the roaring, tossing waves at the edge of the volcano never ceased.

Sometimes a thin blue flame breaks through the cracks or roars up through a chimney at the side. All around the lake is a deposit of 'Pele's hair,' a dun-coloured glassy thread that is always ready to stick into one's hand, with numberless little points. In some places it lies so thick that it looks like a blanket of disagreeable tawny fur.

It is necessary to look out for a sudden

change of wind at Kilauea. I had almost to run one day to escape being stifled with fumes of sulphur, and I picked up a lovely scarlet honeybird which had rashly flown that way and met a sulphurous death.

My last view of the volcano was at night, when its red colour changed to the yellow of a daffodil. Enormous waves and fountains of fire were then playing and flinging up wreaths of spray, which fell almost at my feet and lay like red-hot snakes till they cooled into pitchiness.

While I was there the sky at evening was generally very green, and peculiarly lovely in contrast with the orange of the fire. The calm, nearly level outline of the distant mountain (Mona Loa) and the young tender moon made a delightful relief from the fiery terrors in front of me.

I left Kilauea feeling that I had seen one of the most wonderful sights that the world contains, and I had learnt the lesson that even a lake of fire can be beautiful.

CHAPTER V

OUR NEXT DUTY

IT is earnestly to be desired that legislation as to leprosy in India should be the practical outcome of the sympathy called forth by Father Damien's life and death. There can be no doubt that public opinion on the question is very different now from what it was a few years ago.

Nevertheless, from observations made during my six months' tour in India, I am convinced that public opinion concerning it is still far from what it ought to be. We are only half-awake to a great evil and a great shame. And unless we are speedily roused to active measures it would not be rash to prophesy that, instead of having it brought before us as it has recently been brought before the medical faculty of Paris, it will be brought home to us as it has been brought home to the people of Natal and Queensland. In both these places the invasion of leprosy has driven the inhabitants, in self-defence, to summon public meetings and call upon the authorities to act at once and isolate the infected.

It is natural but rather sad that people should be resigned to the fact of 250,000 of our fellow-subjects dying of leprosy, but tremendously agitated when they find that there is an idea that the mutton chop they have bought in the meat-market may have been handled by a leper.

It is not now necessary for me to refer to the special horrors of the disease, or to discuss the question of its heredity or contagiousness or infectiousness. Enough has already been said for public information on these points. It is now generally known that the children and descendants of lepers frequently become lepers either by way of inheritance or by direct infection from their parents. It is also undeniable that healthy persons— natives and even Europeans, who are beyond the suspicion of hereditary taint—if they continually associate with lepers, are liable to contract the disease, either by involuntary inoculation or by other means. The case of Father Damien is fresh in our minds, and he told me that he had noted many other cases of persons who had come in perfect health to Molokai, and who, after residing there for some time, had become lepers. I saw in the prison at Honolulu a man named Keanu who had committed a murder, and who had consented to be inoculated from a leper by Dr. Arnim five years ago, in consideration of his death-sentence being commuted. He was a strong, healthy man, with no hereditary taint, and he has now become a confirmed leper.

Surely the Government need not delay action till it has been decided exactly how leprosy is propagated. Is it not enough to know that in *some* way it is communicated by its victims to the outside world? My own belief is that heredity, contagion (under certain conditions), inhalation, and inoculation are all four means of its spreading. But whether or not this be so, the fact is undeniable that it does spread wherever there is no segregation, and that it decreases and finally comes to an end (as in our own country) where segregation is carefully practised.

My object now is to tell briefly what I saw and heard last year in India, and to propose a simple remedy. My route lay by Ceylon and Madras to Calcutta, and thence to the districts of Nuddeah Zillah and Santhalia, where I visited about thirty villages, proceeding thence to the leper-stricken city of Ranigunj, with its attendant villages, Mejia and Kushti.

Then I went to the leading cities in the North-west Provinces, and afterwards to the Punjaub and Cashmere, visiting Bombay on my way home, and making the acquaintance there of Dr. Vandyke Carter, the great authority on leprosy. During this tour I found lepers in almost every town and village on my route, even though my stay in the place might be only of a few hours' duration.

The official report gives 135,000 as the existing number of lepers in India, but there can be little doubt that they already exceed 250,000, and that their numbers are steadily growing. Nor can this growth be wondered at, for however the disease is propagated it has every opportunity of increasing.

I saw most ghastly lepers begging in the streets and in the balconies of houses. I met them at railway stations and in places of public resort. In one small bazaar a friend of mine told me he had just counted twelve. I even heard of one who was employed by an English baker in the making of bread.

Mr. Gilford of Tarantarn informs me that

a leper is the cook in one of the railway restaurants in the Punjaub, and that he wears a glove to conceal the fact when serving his customers.

It is, moreover, estimated that all the copper money in India has passed through the hands of lepers. I found in Bombay a man whose hands were covered with leprosy engaged in the railway service as a ticket-collector. Who can estimate the danger to the English and native community of many hundreds of railway tickets daily passing through this man's hands? An English lady in the same city had, just before my arrival, fallen a victim to the disease, to her extreme horror.

Lepers, with their revolting miseries fully exposed, associate freely with the community. They marry when they choose; they love a roving life, and thus continually become fresh centres for propagating the disease.

I was assured by Mr. MacGuire, the superintendent of the Leper Asylum in Calcutta, that he could testify, from often-repeated observations, that in the congregations of poor people who assemble at the funeral feasts of the wealthy natives, one person in three was a leper. By the same authority I was told that the asylum was generally overcrowded, and that the police do not hesitate to bring in cabs lepers who are in a dying state, and for whom it is necessary to turn out some less imminent cases.

Indeed the evil is so widespread that—as Lord Dufferin said to me—one might almost as readily undertake to rid India of its snakes as of its leprosy. Moreover, the absence of Indian public opinion on such matters, and the constitutional callousness of the native mind, increase the difficulty in a way that English readers can scarcely estimate. So careless of danger does fatalism make men to this evil that, in the great leper hospital at Tarantarn, the authorities—as I was assured by an official there—have to hunt out relatives of the deceased, who have come in pretending that they are leprous, and who are actually willing to become infected for the sake of acquiring board, lodging, and the power of living an idle life. The Indian desires above all things to be a man of money, and what the leper at Tarantarn likes is to save two out of the three rupees allowed him monthly, and either to hide them in the ground, put them out at interest, or invest them in jewelry for his wife. One man had thus .acquired 600 rupees—at the cost of most wretched diet, and consequent increase of the disease.

The following extract is from the report in the *Bombay Gazette* of the 6th April 1889 of a meeting of the Bombay Municipal Corporation held on the previous Thursday. I have suppressed some of the painful details, and I feel that only the importance of the subject could justify the introduction of what I have left. I am thankful to say that an important committee (with the Prince of Wales as President) has just been formed, of which one object is to inquire into the question of leprosy in India. Much interesting information may also be got by applying to Mr. Wellesley Bailey, of 17 Glengyle Terrace, Edinburgh, who is the excellent Secretary of a Mission to Lepers Society.

'An important debate took place on a

notice of motion by Mr. T. B. Kirkham, calling attention to the defective regulation of persons affected with leprosy in Bombay, and requesting the Municipal Commissioner to report what additional powers, if any, were required by the Health Department to enable it to deal effectively with the evil.

'Mr. Kirkham said that a few weeks ago, in the discharge of his official duties, he had occasion to visit the Elphinstone High School and the St. Xavier's College, both large educational institutions, and he found to his astonishment that for some months a colony of lepers had taken up their abode on the flagstones surrounding the large Nacoda Tank, which lay between the two institutions, and that the authorities of these two institutions, notwithstanding their appeals to the police and to the Health Department, found themselves practically unable to dislodge the people from these places. The Rev. Dr. Meyer, the Principal of the St. Xavier's College, took him round and pointed out to him these people on the borders of the tank, performing their ablutions in the middle of the day, and he saw them with his own eyes dressing their terrible sores with stones lying about them, and then flinging away those stones, to be picked up or trodden upon by any one. Dr. Meyer told him that he had seen these unfortunate people with his own eyes rubbing their leprous sores on the iron railings surrounding the Elphinstone High School, and had seen boys let loose from the school a few minutes afterwards sitting on these very railings, occasionally, it might be, with bare feet. Being asked what the police had done in the matter, Dr. Meyer replied that, with every desire to assist, the police had been unable practically to do anything, and that a day or two after these men were dislodged from their abode, they again came back to the place. In reply to a representation of the Principal of the Elphinstone School, Dr. Weir, the Health Officer, said that he sympathised with him, but regretted there was nothing in the Municipal Act that empowered him to interfere in the matter. That was a most extraordinary letter to emanate from the Health Department of a great city to a public official in charge of thousands of boys, informing him that the department was utterly powerless to interfere in the matter. He thought it his duty to ask whether it was safe and proper that these people should be allowed to go about and do what they pleased within a few yards of some two thousand young men. It might be called the artificial propagation of leprosy. He was sure the Corporation would not deem it a satisfactory settlement of the question even if these poor people, when driven away from the Esplanade, were simply to take refuge in some less known parts of the town.

'Dr. Arnott said that the subject of leprosy had attracted the attention of the profession for a very long time. If there was any authority on the disease who deserved respectful attention that was Dr. Vandyke Carter, and he had over and over again urged the pressing necessity of providing suitable asylums for lepers, and taking measures to prevent their being a danger to the community. Some refuge must be provided for them. At present the only places where they could live were a small dhuramshala at

Byculla, a small ward at the Sir Jamsetjee Hospital, and the asylum at Trombay. With these exceptions there was in Bombay no place, no refuge, no asylum, where these poor creatures might go and might be cared for.

'Mr. Dosabhoy Framjee said he had very often seen lepers sitting in front of the Girgaum Police Court in company with other healthy people. The worst of it was that lepers went to places where articles of food were sold, and sometimes they stood there for hours, and would not go away until alms were given them.

'Mr. Bomanjee Pestonjee Master said that from what he could gather from the remarks of the much respected councillor, Mr. Kirkham, even the police had no power to deal with the evil, and their only resource was to request Government, through their President, to enact a measure by which these people could be segregated, the Corporation paying for the building of an asylum and for its maintenance.

'Dr. Blaney said that every year he gave as Coroner orders for disposing of the dead bodies of ten, twelve, or fifteen lepers. He did not hold a regular inquest on them, but always made his inquiries, and he found that some of them had died on the road-side, sometimes in front of the Elphinstone College, and sometimes at one or other of the wells on the Esplanade. Some of them drowned themselves in these wells, tired of life.

'He said he did not think there was a single well on the Esplanade in which a leper was not drowned. All over Bombay, in dark corners, in gullies, where rats and bandicoots had taken their abode, these lepers were hiding themselves, thrown out by their families, to pine away neglected and forlorn. Lepers were to be seen in all parts of the city, and not at the Elphinstone School and the St. Xavier's College alone.'

I should be the last to advise the bringing so painful a matter before the public if there were not a remedy. But I believe there is one, and it is simple, if only the indifference of public opinion can be overcome. For whatever is done must be begun in England, and officially begun; then it will be worked out in India, and there can be little doubt that large sums of money would be given by rich native gentlemen as soon as they felt the pressure of Government's authority and approval.

And the most speedy and practical way in

which this result could be effected seems to me to be this:—

That the Supreme Government should enact: 1. That (local self-government having become the rule) each district should have a leper asylum in its district town (where already two medical officers—a European and a native—reside in the district hospital), and that the cost of the maintenance of the lepers should be met by their municipalities and district boards, assisted perhaps by private benevolence. It would be no great hardship that each village should thus be called upon to support in an asylum the lepers who already subsist on its alms. 2. That any leprous person being found without any ostensible means of support should be taken by the police to the nearest civil surgeon for examination, and that the police should then have power, with the surgeon's certificate, to bring him before a magistrate, who should be empowered to confine him in the nearest asylum, to be detained there till further order of the court. (At present lepers go in and out of hospitals just when they choose.)

Such an Act is already in force with regard to lunatics, and the case of lepers is far more pressing.

The Act would only touch vagrant begging lepers, but it is they who are the greatest danger to the community; and if this much-needed and *comparatively* inexpensive reform could be effected, others would doubtless follow, and in an appreciable time our Indian Empire might be rid of the terrible scourge of leprosy.

From our own land (which had formerly

250 leper hospitals) it has been banished by careful segregation and wise sanitary measures. In Norway the Government, with a revenue of about a million, has not hesitated to legislate to such good purpose that in thirty years the number of home cases of leprosy has decreased 75 per cent. In every place where segregation has been enforced the plague has been stayed.

The present moment is the time for every man and woman who feels our responsibility towards India and towards humanity at large to push this matter by all the influence and all the money they can command.

The Prince of Wales's fine speech at the first meeting of the Committee of the 'Father Damien' Memorial Fund at Marlborough House will have been read by thousands, but I cannot do better than subjoin a portion of it after the prospectus of the Society.

The 'Father Damien' Memorial Fund.

The death of Father Damien, completing his noble sacrifice of himself for his brother-men, has suggested the thought that the sympathy of the United Kingdom ought to find expression in a substantial memorial of his work. Such a memorial may most fitly take the form of—

1. A monument to Father Damien on the spot at Molokai where his remains are interred. (Moved by Mr. EDWARD CLIFFORD and seconded by the DUKE OF WESTMINSTER.)

2. The construction of a leper ward in London, probably in connection with some London hospital or school, to be called the Father Damien Ward;[1] and the endowment of a travel-

---

[1] It seems possible that the first part of this resolution will be carried out in the spirit rather than in the letter, by arrangement of some kind being made for the due care and treatment of any lepers in Great Britain.

ling studentship or studentships to encourage the study of leprosy. (Moved by SIR JAMES PAGET and seconded by Mr. J. HUTCHINSON.)

3. A full and complete inquiry into the question of leprosy in India, one of the chief seats of the disease, where there are about 250,000 lepers, and no adequate means of dealing with the evil. In accordance with the recommendation recently put forth by the Royal College of Physicians it will probably be necessary to send out a Commission to India, in order to discover the steps that should be taken to alleviate, and if possible to eradicate, the disease. (Moved by SIR W. GUYER HUNTER and seconded by CARDINAL MANNING.)

President of the Committee.
H.R.H. THE PRINCE OF WALES.

Committee.
THE ARCHBISHOP OF CANTERBURY.
THE DUKE OF NORFOLK, K.G.
THE DUKE OF WESTMINSTER, K.G.
THE MARQUIS OF HARTINGTON.
THE MARQUIS OF DUFFERIN AND AVA, G.C.S.I.
THE EARL OF DERBY, K.G.
THE EARL OF CARNARVON.
THE EARL OF ROSEBERY.
GENERAL VISCOUNT WOLSELEY, G.C.B.
LORD RANDOLPH S. CHURCHILL, M.P.

Baron Ferdinand Rothschild, M.P.
The Bishop of London.
Dr. Vaughan, Bishop of Salford.
The Hon. G. Curzon, M.P.
The Right Hon. W. E. Gladstone, M.P.
The Right Hon. The Lord Mayor.
The Right Hon. John Morley, M.P.
General Sir J. Lintorn Simmons, G.C.B.
Col. Sir Edward Bradford, K.C.S.I.
Sir Alfred Lyall, K.C.B.
Cardinal Manning.
Sir William Mackinnon, Bart.
Sir A. Borthwick, M.P.
Sir R. Temple, G.C.S.I., M.P.
Sir George Stokes, Bart., M.P.
Sir Joseph Fayrer, K.C.S.I.
Sir William Jenner, Bart., K.C.B.
Sir James Paget, Bart.
R. Thorne Thorne, M.D.
Sir W. Guyer Hunter, K.C.M.G., M.P.
Sir W. MacCormac.
Sir Charles U. Aitchison, K.C.S.I.
Jonathan Hutchinson, Esq.
Rev. C. H. Spurgeon.
Principal Fairbairn.
W. S. Lilly, Esq.
A. Walter, Esq.
E. Lawson, Esq.
Frank Harris, Esq.
E. Clifford, Esq.

Honorary Secretaries.

Frank Harris, Esq. | Rev. Hugh Chapman.
Robson Roose, M.D.

The Prince of Wales, in opening the proceedings, said : 'The heroic life and death of Father Damien has not only roused the sympathy of the United Kingdom, but it has gone deeper—it has brought home to us that the circumstances of our vast Indian and Colonial Empire oblige us, in a measure at least, to follow his example; and this not for foreigners and strangers, but for our own fellow-subjects. India with its 250,000 lepers, and our Colonies with their unnumbered but increasing victims to a loathsome disease, that has hitherto baffled medical skill, have a far stronger claim on our aid than the poor natives of the Hawaiian Islands could ever have had on the young Belgian priest who has given his life for them. To mark our debt to him, as well as our sympathy with his noble self-sacrifice, I have to propose to this Committee a memorial scheme that embraces a threefold object. . . .

'There can, I think, be no question whatever as to the advisability of the second proposal contained in this part of the scheme. I mean a special endowment to promote the study of leprosy, which should take the form of travelling studentships, and thereby render the metropolis the centre from which to promote the scientific study and investigation of this insidious disease. Let me here remind the Committee that leprosy has shown itself, and seems to be spreading, in our South African and Australian Colonies, while in some of our Colonial possessions its ravages are almost unchecked. This leads me naturally to the third part of this memorial scheme—a full and complete inquiry into the question of leprosy in India. Since the well-

known report of the Royal College of
Physicians of 1867, drawn up after extensive
inquiry carried out under the Duke of
Newcastle, at the instigation of the Governor
of the Windward Islands, there has been no
similar general report following a special
inquiry embracing the leprous countries of
the world. But the immediate result of this
report of 1867 was a decision of the Government enjoining the repeal of all legislative
enactments in the Empire for the compulsory
segregation of lepers. And it must be
remembered that whilst leprosy has been and
is steadily increasing, probably in India, and
certainly in our Colonies, it has steadily
decreased since 1867 in Norway from over
2000 to less than 700 cases, and this decrease
is attributed by specialists to the Government
measures for isolation which have been there

put in force. These measures include compulsory segregation, and have been adopted at a cost of £20,000 a year, although the leper population of Norway now under treatment numbers, as I have said, barely 700 souls. How far segregation should enter into any scheme that may hereafter be adopted to cope with leprosy in the British Empire, it is not for me to say now. But this I may say, the need for renewed investigation into the whole question of leprosy and its contagiousness has become so pressing, owing to professional and other representations as to the increase and communicability of the disease received from all parts of the world, that the Leprosy Committee of the Royal College of Physicians in their recently issued report to the college have urged in the strongest manner possible that the "Government should institute a full and careful scientific investigation of a question which in the interests of humanity calls for immediate attention." It has been thought that private philanthropy should undertake this mission; nor do I doubt that if this Committee puts its hand to the work the objects set forth in the report from which I have read will perhaps be more speedily and thoroughly attained than if they were entrusted to already overburdened Government officials' (cheers).

When Father Damien consecrated his life to Christ and buried himself in the leper settlement of Kalawao he little thought that the echoes of his self-sacrifice would not only be the bugle call to quicken the divine life in thousands of souls who lived under grayer clouds than the rich skies of Molokai hold, but that they would rouse an Empire to rid its neglected myriads of the terrible plague which has last laid him to rest under his palm-tree. But so it is. No one can measure the results of the simplest action performed with a single eye from love to God and man.

> Blow, bugle, blow, set the wild echoes flying,
> Blow, bugle; answer, echoes, dying, dying, dying.
>
> . . . . .
>
> O love, they die in yon rich sky,
>   They faint on hill or field or river:
> Our echoes roll from soul to soul,
>   And grow for ever and for ever.
> Blow, bugle, blow, set the wild echoes flying;
> And answer, echoes, answer, dying, dying, dying.

THE END

Printed by R. & R. CLARK, *Edinburgh*

www.ingramcontent.com/pod-product-compliance
Lightning Source LLC
Chambersburg PA
CBHW020246170426
43202CB00008B/241